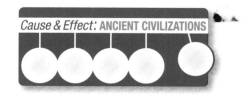

Cause & Effect:
Ancient China

John Allen

San Diego, CA

About the Author
John Allen is a writer who lives in Oklahoma City.

© 2018 ReferencePoint Press, Inc.
Printed in the United States

For more information, contact:
ReferencePoint Press, Inc.
PO Box 27779
San Diego, CA 92198
www.ReferencePointPress.com

LIBRARY OF CONGRESS CATALOGING-IN-PUBLICATION DATA

Name: Allen, John, 1957– author.
Title: Cause & Effect. Ancient China/by John Allen.
Other titles: Ancient China
Description: San Diego, CA: ReferencePoint Press, Inc., 2018. | Series:
    Cause & Effect: Ancient Civilizations | Includes bibliographical
    references and index. | Audience: Grades 9 to 12.
Identifiers: LCCN 2017001819 (print) | LCCN 2017004548 (ebook) | ISBN
    9781682821480 (hardback) | ISBN 9781682821497 (eBook)
Subjects: LCSH: China—Civilization.
Classification: LCC DS721 .A48 2018 (print) | LCC DS721 (ebook) | DDC
    931--dc23
LC record available at https://lccn.loc.gov/2017001819

CONTENTS

"History is a complex study of the many causes that have influenced happenings of the past and the complicated effects of those varied causes."

—William & Mary School of Education,
Center for Gifted Education

Understanding the causes and effects of historical events and time periods is rarely simple. The largest and most influential empire of ancient India, for instance, came into existence largely because of a series of events set in motion by Persian and Greek invaders. Although the Mauryan Empire was both wealthy and well organized and benefited enormously from strong rulers and administrators, the disarray sowed by invading forces created an opening for one of India's most ambitious and successful ancient rulers—Chandragupta, the man who later came to be known in the West as the "Indian Julius Caesar." Had conditions in India at the time been different, the outcome might have been something else altogether.

The value of analyzing cause and effect in the context of ancient civilizations, therefore, is not necessarily to identify a single cause for a singular event. The real value lies in gaining a greater understanding of that civilization as a whole and being able to recognize the many factors that gave shape and direction to its rise, its development, its fall, and its lasting importance. As outlined by the National Center for History in the Schools at the University of California–Los Angeles, these factors include "the importance of the individual in history . . . the influence of ideas, human interests, and beliefs; and . . . the role of chance, the accidental and the irrational."

ReferencePoint's Cause & Effect: Ancient Civilizations series examines some of the world's most interesting and important civilizations by focusing on various causes and consequences. For instance, in *Cause & Effect: Ancient India*, a chapter explores how one Indian ruler helped transform Buddhism into a world religion. And in *Cause & Effect: Ancient Egypt*, one chapter delves into the importance of the Nile River in the development of Egyptian civilization. Every book in the series includes thoughtful discussion of questions like these—supported by facts, examples, and a mix of fully documented primary and secondary source quotes. Each title also includes an overview of the civilization so that readers have a broad context for understanding the more detailed discussions of causes and their effects.

The value of such study is not limited to the classroom; it can also be applied to many areas of contemporary life. The ability to analyze and interpret history's causes and consequences is a form of critical thinking. Critical thinking is crucial in many professions, ranging from law enforcement to science. Critical thinking is also essential for developing an educated citizenry that fully understands the rights and obligations of living in a free society. The ability to sift through and analyze complex processes and events and identify their possible outcomes enables people in that society to make important decisions.

The Cause & Effect: Ancient Civilizations series has two primary goals. One is to help students think more critically about the human societies that once populated our world and develop a true understanding of their complexities. The other is to help build a foundation for those students to become fully participating members of the society in which they live.

IMPORTANT EVENTS IN THE HISTORY OF ANCIENT CHINA

1600–1046 BCE
The Shang dynasty develops a sophisticated writing system and begins producing bronze tools.

1046 BCE
The Zhou dynasty, the longest in Chinese history, rises to power.

214 BCE
Qin Shi Huang links and extends sections of the Great Wall.

BCE **1500**   **1100**   **600**   **100**

551 BCE
The philosopher Kongfuzi, also known as Confucius, is born.

135 BCE
Han envoy Zhang Qian opens new trade routes to the west along the Silk Road.

480 BCE
Sun Tzu writes *The Art of War*, a treatise on warfare.

221 BCE
Qin Shi Huang unifies China and takes the throne as first emperor.

1045
Chinese inventor Bi Sheng creates a movable-type system for printing.

1279
Mongol emperor Kublai Khan assumes the throne.

460
Northern Wei ruler supports Buddhism with carved cliff shrines.

105
A Chinese official named Zai Lun starts an industry to make paper.

850
Chinese alchemists rediscover the recipe for gunpowder.

CE **100**   **600**   **1100**   **1600**

590
Emperor Wendi builds a vast canal system that extends through central Asia.

1024
The first paper money is printed in Chengdu, Sichuan, and goes into wide use.

1644
The Ming dynasty falls to non-Chinese Manchu invaders.

626
Under Emperor Taizong, the Silk Road trade flourishes.

1405
Ming emperor Yongle builds iconic Great Wall sections of stone and earth, with signal towers and trenches.

1912
China becomes a democratic republic, ending the imperial period.

The Terra-Cotta Army

On a March day in 1974 Chinese farmers digging a well in Shaanxi Province uncovered pieces of terra-cotta statues buried in the ground. This find led to the most amazing excavation of the twentieth century. Chinese archaeologists unearthed a terra-cotta army, an array of thousands of life-size terra-cotta figures. The statues surrounded the tomb of the Emperor Qin Shi Huang in a reconstruction of the ruler's imperial palace complete with carefully modeled warriors in battle garb, archers with crossbows, servants, acrobats, and entertainers. The figures in the terra-cotta army, dating from before 210 BCE, the date of the emperor's death, are rendered in astonishing variety and detail. Their discovery caused historians and archaeologists to reexamine their views about ancient China and how its civilization has affected the world.

Preparing for the Afterlife

The excavation shows that Qin Shi Huang, the first great emperor of China, spared no expense in preparing for the afterlife. Qin had achieved great successes in his reign. "Qin Shi Huangdi may have conquered China with his army," writes historian Arthur Lubow, "but he held it together with a civil administration system that endured for centuries. Among other accomplishments, the emperor standardized weights and measures and introduced a uniform writing script."[1] He also built new canals and roads to link Chinese cities and constructed the first sections of what would become the Great Wall. Qin's tomb is thus a monument to himself, begun shortly after he seized the imperial throne. Reportedly more than seven hundred thousand workers toiled on the project for three decades, until rebellions brought it to an end a year after Qin's death.

> "[Emperor] Qin Shi Huangdi may have conquered China with his army, but he held it together with a civil administration system that endured for centuries."[1]
>
> —Historian Arthur Lubow

Besides the importance of religious belief, the terra-cotta army excavation revealed how sophisticated and well organized the methods of manufacture were in ancient China. The amount of raw materials and number of kilns necessary for the project had to be enormous. The terra-cotta figures were produced by assembly line, apparently with an ancient version of the conveyor belt system used by automobile makers today. Bodies were each assembled from two molds—front and back sections for human figures, left and right sections for horses. Heads and limbs were modeled separately, providing for endless variations in facial expressions and gestures.

Farmers digging a well in China unearthed this army of terra-cotta soldiers in 1974. Numbering in the thousands, the statues surrounded the tomb of Emperor Qin Shi Huang.

This attention to detail suggests the importance of individuals, even in a military setting. The tomb figures, with their variety of mustaches, beards, caps, and hairstyles, depict an army of soldiers and support personnel drawn from every corner of the empire. The army also reflects the hierarchy of command, with each officer figure a few inches taller than the common foot soldiers. Details of dress reflect each figure's military task. Infantry wear the riveted armor vests of hand-to-hand fighters. The archer figures are modeled with studs on the soles of their shoes to prevent slipping when launching their arrows. Overall, Emperor Qin's tomb complex and terra-cotta army represent a combination of power, piety, ingenuity, and creative energy that marked the dynasties of ancient China.

Important Inventions

The empire of China spanned more than two thousand years, from the third century BCE to the early twentieth century. During that time, as regimes alternated between periods of unity and rebellion, the creative spark of the Chinese produced dozens of important inventions and new technologies. During the second century BCE, technicians in the landlocked province of Szechuan created a drilling method to extract saltwater—and later natural gas—from deep in the earth. Around 105 CE an official of the Han court developed a process of pounding a mixture of mulberry tree fibers, rags, and fishnets into pulp to make paper. In 132 CE Zhang Heng made the first seismograph, a device that measured the direction of an earthquake. Around the same time, Chinese alchemists stumbled on the formula for gunpowder, which was used for making fireworks and firearms. Artisans in the Tang dynasty perfected the craft of making fine porcelain—often called china in the West—and a whole commercial industry arose around porcelain production. During the Song dynasty of the Middle Ages, the Chinese used lodestone, which aligns with the earth's magnetic fields, to make a compass for navigation. The ancient Chinese also invented everyday items that people around the world take for granted, such as the kite, the umbrella, and the wheelbarrow. They even developed the ideas for paper money and restaurants.

Chinese inventions circulated by means of the Silk Road, a trade route westward from China all the way to Europe. This introduced the first stirrings of what is now called globalization—a mingling of cultures and commerce. Merchants of the time not only traded goods but also took part in a sophisticated cultural exchange. "The traveling merchants and officials wanted to eat the cuisine that they were used to in their local region," says Robin D.S. Yates, a professor of history and East Asian Studies at McGill University in Montreal. "And people with some extra wealth in the urban centers also wanted to try food from different regions. So what developed was a new urban type of culture that included eating out in restaurants and the drinking of tea."[2]

The history of China offers many lessons about conquest and peaceful exchange, prejudice and tolerance, openness and isolation. Today China must confront many of these issues in its relations with the West and with its neighbor countries. Ancient China's profound effect on modern civilization, from philosophical ideas to crucial inventions, is still unfolding today.

> "People with some extra wealth in the urban centers also wanted to try food from different regions. So what developed was a new urban type of culture that included eating out in restaurants and the drinking of tea."[2]
>
> —Robin D.S. Yates, professor of history and East Asian Studies at McGill University

CHAPTER ONE

A Brief History of Ancient China

China is one of the major ancient civilizations of the world, with a written history that dates back to the Shang dynasty thirty-six hundred years ago. (Among the other ancient civilizations are the Mesopotamian, Egyptian, Indus Valley, Aztec, and Greco-Roman civilizations.) No other nation can trace its history back in an unbroken line as China can. The Chinese empire, which was first consolidated under the Qin dynasty more than two thousand years ago, survived until the overthrow of the last emperor and the institution of a republic in 1912. Western visitors, beginning with the thirteenth-century Venetian merchant Marco Polo, returned to Europe with stories of China's natural beauty, fabulous wealth, and extensive culture. The customs and beliefs of the Chinese people—including ideas about government, society, family, and personal conduct based on the teachings of the philosopher Confucius—were passed down largely intact for centuries, from the beginning of the imperial period up to the present day. This adherence to tradition ensures that the civilization of ancient China continues to affect Chinese life and thought.

The Beginnings of Chinese Civilization

Ancient Chinese civilization began more than four thousand years ago with a number of city-states in the Yellow River valley. The Yellow River (Huang He), known also as China's mother river, zigzags for more than 2,900 miles (4,667 km), from Mongolia to the Pacific Ocean. It is China's second-longest river after the Yangtze. Rich yellow silt in the river's southern bend made for ideal farmland, especially in a nation where only 10 percent of the land is fertile. Its frequent floods, with their toll on people and crops, also earned it the reputation of being China's sorrow. Dozens of ethnic groups and nomadic peoples settled in the Yellow River valley and took up agriculture. Archaeologists have found pottery, tools of stone and bronze, and other artifacts from these early cultures in many sites along the river.

The Xia dynasty was the first to emerge, around 2200 BCE. The founding Xia emperor was Yu, formerly an adviser to local sages. Yu introduced flood controls and launched a dynasty that made strides in agriculture, craftwork in jade and bronze, and commodity trading. The Xia also created a calendar based on the movements of the sun and moon. Five hundred years of Xia rule ended with the reign of Jie, a notorious tyrant. Tang, the leader of a rival tribe, marshaled the disgruntled subjects to overthrow Jie around 1600 BCE.

Tang founded the Shang dynasty, which thrived in the Yellow River valley in northern China from about 1600 to 1046 BCE. The Shang farmed, hunted, and raised livestock for food. Shang soldiers fought frequently with neighboring tribes and nomads, and the Shang capital was

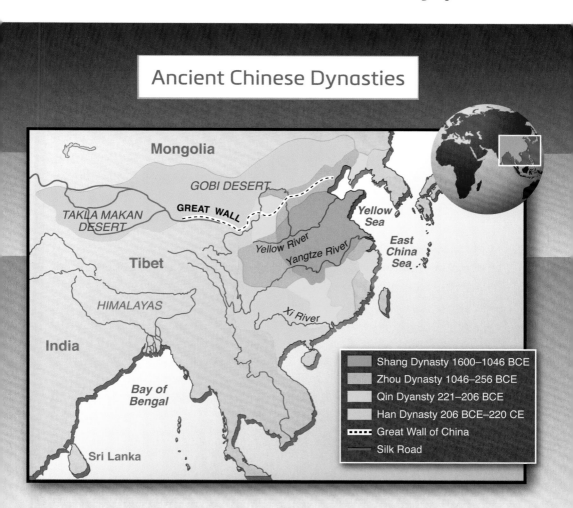

Ancient Chinese Dynasties

Mongolia

GOBI DESERT

GREAT WALL

TAKLA MAKAN DESERT

Yellow Sea

Tibet

Yellow River

Yangtze River

East China Sea

HIMALAYAS

Xi River

India

Bay of Bengal

Sri Lanka

Shang Dynasty 1600–1046 BCE
Zhou Dynasty 1046–256 BCE
Qin Dyansty 221–206 BCE
Han Dynasty 206 BCE–220 CE
Great Wall of China
Silk Road

moved six times before being permanently settled in Yin around 1350 BCE. The Shang dynasty developed a sophisticated writing system, invented a number of musical instruments, made artistic bronze casts and ceramic pottery, and discovered the planet Mars and certain comets. Its capital at Yin maintained a rich court life, including rituals to placate the spirits. Archaeologists have uncovered thousands of oracle bones, which are pieces of bone and tortoise shells that were inscribed with written messages and then cracked under intense heat to obtain the spirits' verdict. The last Shang ruler was Shang Zhou, who killed himself following his army's defeat at the hands of the rival Zhou people.

The Longest Dynasty

The Zhou dynasty endured longer than any other in Chinese history. It lasted almost eight hundred years, from about 1046 to 256 BCE. The Zhou dynasty can be divided into three periods. The western Zhou period (1046–770 BCE) saw the rise of Zhou rulers who invoked the so-called mandate of heaven, the idea that they ruled by divine right. The mandate supposedly required each leader to rule with justice or else lose support of the supreme god of heaven. In this early period, a loose grouping of city-states became progressively more centralized, giving Zhou rulers greater control over taxation and local governments. Ultimately, however, the ruling clan lost its grip on power and was forced to move eastward to Luoyang in what is today Henan Province.

In the second Zhou period, called the Spring and Autumn Period (770–476 BCE), the empire broke apart into dozens of kingdoms vying for power. (This period was named for a Confucian book of history that described the struggles among local nobles.) There was continual feuding, with fewer than forty peaceful years altogether. During this period a Chinese general named Sun Tzu wrote *The Art of War*, a book that laid out timeless precepts of military strategy, such as "all war is based on deception" and "the supreme art of war is to subdue the enemy without fighting."[3]

> "The supreme art of war is to subdue the enemy without fighting."[3]
>
> —Chinese general Sun Tzu in *The Art of War*

Struggles and fragmentation meant there were many different languages, customs, and cultural beliefs among the various tribes and

A Vast and Varied Land

The history of ancient China is closely linked to its geography. China is a vast and varied land, with extremes of icy mountaintops and blazing deserts among its climate regions. The ancient Chinese settled along the nation's two main rivers—first on the Yellow River in the north and then on the Yangtze in the south. The Yangtze, China's longest river, also became its chief area for growing rice, producing roughly twice the amount of food as the fields along the Yellow River. The headwaters of these two rivers come from melting snows in the mountains to the west, including the Himalayas, which include some of the world's highest peaks. By contrast, the Turpan Depression, a huge trough at the foot of the Bogda Mountains in far western China, is one of the lowest points on Earth, as well as one of China's hottest and most arid areas. The dry climate in Turpan has helped preserve ancient tombs there from as long ago as the western Jin dynasty (265–420 CE).

The monsoon rains blowing north from the Indian Ocean helped create fertile plains in central China. In fact, the most fertile areas of China were isolated from other civilizations by mountains in the west, deserts in the northwest, steppes in the northeast, and dense jungles in the south. This produced a sense among the Chinese of living in their own world, surrounded by nomads and barbarians. Thus, the Chinese empire could develop independently, with its own languages, culture, and political traditions.

clans. This led to an abundance of new ideas and philosophies—the so-called one hundred schools of thought. Confucianism, Taoism, and legalism were among the philosophies that arose and rapidly gained wide influence during this period and the one that followed. Amid the chaos of cultural change and widespread clan warfare, Zhou rulers found themselves reduced to mere figureheads, with scarcely enough troops to defend themselves. During the three centuries of the Spring and Autumn Period, constant fighting finally left only a few main rival groups standing.

Civil war marked the third period of the Zhou dynasty, called the Warring States Period (476–221 BCE). Eight states fought for supremacy during this time. A class of military specialists arose to lead troops armed with cast-metal weapons into battle. Yet this turbulent era also produced great Confucian thinkers who emphasized ethics and an orderly daily life. The structures of government that developed would remain in place for centuries to come. The use of iron tools, fertilizer, and more sophisticated methods of irrigation became common. Eventually the brutal wars produced a single conquering kingdom, the Qin dynasty, which unified China under one emperor, Qin Shi Huang. This was the beginning of imperial China. (*Qin*, pronounced "chin," is the source of China's name.) It was Qin Shi Huang who started to build the Great Wall. He maintained a strong central government based on ideas from legalism that people must be ruled by fear. One of Qin Shi Huang's advisers said of him, "He is merciless, with the heart of a tiger or a wolf."[4] He also had a genius for organization. He streamlined administrative practices and instituted land reforms to boost farming and feed his troops. In later years Qin Shi Huang sought an elixir for immortality and prepared his own fabulous tomb near Xianyang, complete with seven thousand terra-cotta soldiers and other court figures.

> "He is merciless, with the heart of a tiger or a wolf."[4]
>
> —Adviser to Qin Shi Huang, founding emperor of the Qin dynasty

A Model for Later Governments

Qin Shi Huang's death led to a civil war that produced the Han dynasty (206 BCE–220 CE). This dynasty of roughly four hundred years is reckoned by Chinese historians to be a model for later governments, with art, science, politics, and technology all flourishing. The first Han emperor was a commoner and former bandit named Liu Bang who had served as a minor official in the Qin dynasty. When the Qin collapsed, Liu Bang raised an army and managed to seize the vacant throne. As emperor, he set up the capital city of Chang'an in what is now Shaanxi Province in central China. The capital, located at the hub of several major roads, featured palaces, residential areas, and two thriving markets. The city soon became not only the political but also the cultural center of China, with a population of more than a quarter million. Its only rival in size among ancient cities was Rome.

The Han dynasty reached its zenith with the long reign of Emperor Wudi (141–86 BCE). Wudi adopted Confucianism as the official source for rules of personal conduct and the framework for education. Wudi filled his bureaucracy with experts educated in Confucian thought, a practice that carried through to other dynasties down through the centuries. Poetry and literature thrived under Wudi's rule.

Under the reign of Emperor Wudi, the Han dynasty reached its pinnacle in the first and second centuries BCE. This seventeenth-century artwork depicts the emperor being transported out of his palace in a cart.

His government sponsored the historian Sima Qian in writing a vast history of China, including accounts of the barbarian tribes who lived beyond the empire's borders. Wudi's armies expanded these borders by retaking lands in southern China and northern Vietnam. His troops made conquests as far west as the Fergana region in modern Uzbekistan, seizing the fast, long-legged Fergana horses for their value as cavalry mounts. Under Wudi's rule, Han traders controlled important trade routes for silk, gold, wine, wool fabric, and spices.

Wudi's constant wars took their toll after his death. His western Han empire dissolved into factions, and around 25 CE a new capital sprang up at Luoyang in modern Henan Province. The eastern Han rulers were mostly juveniles controlled by relatives and advisers. Politically, this period was marked by rebellion and chaos. Yet the arts thrived, with architecture, stone carving, ceramics, and calligraphy (decorative writing) all reaching new heights of sophistication.

The Three Kingdoms and the Period of Disunion

The collapse of the Han dynasty produced a power vacuum and more than three centuries of fighting for control. Civil wars resulted in the rise of three separate kingdoms, each claiming to possess the mandate of heaven passed on from the Han rulers. The Wei kingdom operated from the former Han capital of Luoyang in the north. It was forged by the former Han poet and warlord Cao Cao and his son Cao Pi.

> "I would rather betray the world than let the world betray me."[5]
>
> —Former Han poet and warlord Cao Cao

Chinese literature portrays Cao Cao as a ruthless tyrant, known for declaring, "I would rather betray the world than let the world betray me."[5] Yet he was also a gifted statesman and military leader. Upon Cao Cao's death, his son took the throne, giving himself the imperial name Wei Wen-di, meaning "Literary Emperor."

In the southwest, in the region of present-day Sichuan, the Shu kingdom arose under the rule of Liu Bei, a warlord descended from the Han emperors. To the south, a general named Sun Quan ruled the Wu kingdom under the name Wu Wudi. Among the three kingdoms, Chinese historians mostly cite the Wei as the legitimate heirs of the Han dynasty. The three kingdoms lasted from 220 to 280 CE, an era marked by warfare and political turmoil. Military strategy advanced with the invention of gunpowder, but overall chaos stifled economic progress in all three kingdoms. More important was the rise of a new aristocracy made up of powerful families who ruled their own fiefdoms.

The three kingdoms eventually gave way to the Jin dynasty (265–420), a failed attempt to reunify China. The three centuries from 280 to 581 are known as the Period of Disunion, which continued the wars and political strife. To deal with daily turmoil, many Chinese turned to Buddhism, which Silk Road merchants from central Asia had brought to China in the first century. Buddhism was a universal religion, accepting followers of any ethnicity or social level. The Chinese saw it as akin to Taoism, with its appeal to a peaceful existence. Buddhist monasteries and temples appeared by the thousands. Around the year 400 a Buddhist leader from central Asia named Kumarajiva led several thousand Chinese monks in Chang'an to translate the major Buddhist texts.

The Period of Disunion also featured wars against nomadic peoples from outside China. The Xianbei, a northern tribe, actually started the northern Wei dynasty (386–534), which drew upon the Chinese culture, employed Chinese officials, and adopted Chinese customs. However, unlike the Romans, who succumbed to barbarian invasions, the Chinese eventually were able to defeat these outsiders and consolidate power under a new dynasty.

From Tyranny to a Golden Age

In 581 Yang Jian, a general in the northern Zhou kingdom, usurped the throne by slaughtering dozens of his relatives. Having already defeated the Qi to establish unity in the north, Yang Jian went on to overrun the weak southern Chen kingdom in Nanjing, thus bringing all of China under his rule. He named himself Wendi, emperor of the Sui dynasty. Like the Qin dynasty, the Sui reign was brief but influential. A small man with a violent temper, Wendi eyed rivals at court with suspicion and ruled China with an iron hand. He focused on spreading Buddhism, restoring Confucian bureaucrats to power, and pursuing huge construction projects and foreign wars. Wendi began work on a vast canal system that eventually extended more than 1,250 miles (2,012 km) through central Asia. Yangdi, Wendi's son and successor, continued the canal project on an even grander scale but fell victim to his own poor judgment. While Yangdi was pursuing disastrous wars in Korea, his kingdom was roiled by rioting peasants angry over heavy taxation. Li Yuan, a northern chieftain, seized the throne from Yangdi's young grandson and proclaimed himself Gaozu, first emperor of the Tang dynasty, in 618.

Emperor Gaozu (pictured) was the first ruler of the Tang dynasty, which Chinese historians consider to be a golden age. Although his reign lasted for only eight years, Gaozu instituted political and economic reform that his successors built upon, resulting in centuries of prosperity and growth.

Chinese historians regard the Tang dynasty (618–907) as a golden age. In the eight years of his reign, Gaozu introduced political and economic reforms that endured throughout the Tang period. He granted amnesty to members of the rival Sui family and kept the most able Sui advisers. Gaozu's son Taizong and the emperors who followed him carried on this program of reform and wise rule. Taizong, beloved by the people for his military exploits before assuming the throne, proved to be an adept administrator. Although he brought great prosperity to China, he lived frugally himself in accordance with Confucian ideas. His military conquests in central Asia led to expanded trade. Under Taizong, China became a world power. His successor, Gaozong, suffered from dizziness and allowed his wife, Wu Zetian, to lead the government. As ancient China's only female ruler, Wu Zetian expanded the kingdom's dominions farther than ever before, establishing contacts with Arabs to the west. Her success in reforming education, taxation, and agriculture make her one of China's greatest rulers.

Emperor Xuanzong carried the Chinese empire to even greater heights. His humane rule included an end to the death penalty and forced conscription of soldiers, improved security on the Silk Road, and financial reforms to shore up the economy. Xuanzong had the laws reframed for clarity and saw to it that they were applied impartially. He boosted commerce by introducing money in standard units keyed to certain commodities such as silk and grain. His reign encouraged innovation, such as new methods of diagnosing disease and the invention of the mechanical clock. However, in his later years, Xuanzong fell in love with his son's wife and began to neglect his responsibilities as emperor. Court intrigues weakened the Tang, leading to armed rebellions that left millions dead. Many of the later Tang emperors abandoned the policies that had been so successful. Wars of revolt led eventually to the fall of the Tang dynasty in 907.

A Peaceful Three Centuries

Once more a violent period descended on China. Five self-styled dynasties battled for dominance, and bandits by the thousands lurked along trading routes and sacked cities for loot. Fifty years after the end of the Tang dynasty, the Song dynasty (960–1279) came together under the emperor Taizu. The eldest son of a northern general, Taizu was practically forced to don the yellow robes of the emperor by mutinous officers. Fortunately for China, Taizu and his descendants proved to be remarkably capable leaders. Unlike the Tang court, which favored military prowess and hunting skills, the Song focused on cultural brilliance, including poetry, landscape painting, calligraphy, and other arts. Wood-block printing reached a peak of perfection, and the invention of movable type increased the number of books in circulation. To maintain good relations with its neighbors, the Song used diplomacy and even bought off potential enemies with payments of tribute. The result was three centuries of peace and stability.

The emperors of the later Song period, known as the southern Song dynasty (1127–1279), retreated to the south and Hangzhou. Invading Mongols finally toppled the Song and ruled as outsiders under the Yuan dynasty. The first Yuan emperor was Kublai Khan, grandson of Genghis Khan. It was Kublai's glittering court at Dadu (now Beijing) that so impressed Marco Polo. Kublai Khan relied on foreign advisers and construction experts in order to lessen the influence of native Chinese bureaucrats. He also allowed religious freedom for Christians and Muslims as well as those who followed traditional Chinese faiths. Later Yuan emperors printed too much of the paper money introduced in Kublai Khan's reign, leading to ruinous inflation and debt. Floods and epidemics, which the people blamed on the Yuan's loss of the mandate of heaven, added to the collapse. A powerful army of native Chinese rebels, called the Red Turbans, managed to oust the Mongol Yuan and seize control of Dadu in 1368.

The Last Great Dynasty

Rebel leader Zhu Yuanzhang restored the line of Han Chinese emperors with the Ming dynasty (1368–1644). Zhu ruled under the name Hongwu, which meant "Vast Magnificent Military." After years of turmoil and natural disasters, the people were relieved when

The Mongols and the Chinese

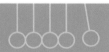

Led by Temujin, the Mongol leader who called himself Genghis Khan ("Universal Ruler"), the Mongols established an empire that stretched from the Sea of Japan to modern Poland and Hungary, an area so vast that China formed only a part of it. Unlike other outsider regimes that seized control of China, the Mongols were little inclined to adopt Chinese ways. The Mongols and the Chinese remained fundamentally different in customs and attitudes.

Their differences often boiled down to the Mongols' reliance on military organization versus the Chinese focus on civil society and family ties. All males in Mongol society served at least some time in the military. Nomadic life accustomed Mongols to move constantly and adapt to local conditions. Unlike the Chinese, Mongol clans had loose family links and depended instead on the imperial code founded by Genghis to decide questions of succession and inheritance. The Mongols considered the native Chinese to be the lowest of the hierarchy of peoples in China, lacking in strength and vigor, with too much emphasis on the written word. The Mongols had little respect for Chinese traditions, even abolishing civil service exams, China's prized method of recruiting talented officials. For their part, the Chinese looked down on the Mongols as filthy barbarians—unwashed, lacking in manners, interested only in power and plunder. Yet these so-called barbarians had a great influence. "They searched for what worked best," says one modern historian, "and when they found it, they spread it to other countries."

Quoted in DiploFoundation, "Genghis Khan and the Making of the Modern World," book review. www.diplomacy.edu.

Hongwu focused on supporting agriculture and rebuilding canals and reservoirs. The emperor brought back traditional Chinese customs that appealed to his own peasant background. Hongwu's reign was often cruel and repressive, but his changes brought prosperity. Hongwu's fourth son, Yongle, also proved an able ruler. He built the Forbidden City, a walled complex of palaces and gardens inside Beijing. Yongle's successors relied on foreign trade and gave great latitude

> "The major problem with an absolute emperor had been recognized long before the Ming dynasty. Concentrating power in the hands of the emperor would spell disaster if the emperor were incompetent or disinterested in government."[6]
>
> —Historian Richard Hooker

to private merchants. As merchants and farmers grew more prosperous, the lines of social class blurred, leading to a more equal society. Nonetheless, later Ming emperors could not prevent decline. "The major problem with an absolute emperor had been recognized long before the Ming dynasty," writes historian Richard Hooker. "Concentrating power in the hands of the emperor would spell disaster if the emperor were incompetent or disinterested in government."[6] Uprisings and natural disasters—including the Little Ice Age, a period of unusual cold—once more weakened the dynasty in power. The Ming, China's last great dynasty, fell to armies of non-Chinese Manchu invaders in 1644. The Manchu set up the Qing dynasty. Qing emperors managed to face down a series of rebellions over the next two centuries, but they followed a disastrous policy of refusing foreign trade and resisting contact with the outside world. In 1912 the Qing finally ceded power to a democratic republic led by Sun Yatsen, bringing the ancient Chinese empire to an end.

How Important Was the Great Wall in the Development of Ancient Chinese Civilization?

Focus Questions

1. Do you think the people of ancient China regarded the Great Wall with feelings of pride? Why or why not?
2. What do you think the building of the Great Wall indicates about ancient China's relationship with the outside world? Explain your answer.
3. What effect did the Great Wall have on activities such as trade and agriculture?

In a conceit made for Hollywood, actor Matt Damon, as a foreign mercenary in medieval China, stands atop the Great Wall alongside Chinese troops, intent on repelling an invading horde—not enemy soldiers but mythological monsters. The big-budget film *The Great Wall*, a US-China collaboration directed by Zhang Yimou, trades on the iconic status of the wall, one of the world's most recognizable landmarks. The Great Wall itself is not only an amazing feat of construction but also a symbol of China's imperial past—for both East and West. On his historic 1972 visit to China, American president Richard Nixon said, "It exceeds all expectations. When one stands there and sees the Wall going to the peak of this mountain and realizes that it runs for hundreds of miles, as a matter of fact thousands of miles, . . . I think that you would have to conclude that this is a great wall and that it had to be built by a great people."[7] Chinese rulers collaborated down the ages to build the wall as a protection against invaders—soldiers, not monsters—and as a boundary enclosing Chinese beliefs and customs.

It offers a glimpse of how the ancient Chinese saw themselves and the sometimes hostile world beyond.

The Longest Wall in the World

The Great Wall of China is one of the greatest architectural achievements in history. It is the longest wall in the world, a series of stone and earth fortifications winding through northern China for more than 13,000 miles (20,921 km) across rugged terrain and steep mountains. Its Chinese name, Changcheng, means "Long Wall." The Great Wall extends from Jiayuguan in the northwestern province of Gansu to Shanhaiguan on the east coast. The wall's actual length is perhaps 1,000 miles (1,609 km) greater still since it loops and doubles back on itself across the passes. Its height varies in different sections from 26 feet (8 m) to 46 feet (14 m). Its base measures more than 30 feet (9 m) in width. Its ramparts (the walkways atop the broad walls) allowed five horses to travel along them side by side. There are more than twenty-five hundred watchtowers along the wall's length, providing a view of the frontier and archery windows from which to shoot arrows at enemy soldiers. Fortresses were built at vulnerable strategic points where attacks were most likely to occur. These were fitted with fortified gatehouses that could not be breached. Nonetheless, as historian Ann Paludan notes, the wall was more than just a means of holding out enemies. "The wall marked the limits of the civilized world," writes Paludan. "The character for wall and city is the same in China and carries the idea of a dividing line or enclosure. Early Chinese walled cities were not built for defensive purposes but for administrative reasons, separating city from field."[8] Construction of the wall occurred in different parts of China at different times, involving many dynasties and a long line of emperors. Overall, its history covers more than twenty-three hundred years.

> "The wall marked the limits of the civilized world."[8]
>
> —Historian Ann Paludan

The Beginnings of the Great Wall

Close attention to Chinese history shows that construction of the Great Wall had more to do with peace than war. Quite often its expansion was an attempt to preserve Chinese culture, boost the economy, and achieve goals of foreign policy. Indeed, the Great Wall is not a single construction but a number of regional walls added to and connected by later dynasties. According to the history journal *China Heritage Quarterly*, "What is promoted in China as a contiguous

Chinese leaders built the Great Wall (pictured) in hopes of preserving their culture and way of life. The wall was intended to separate the civilized world—China—from all others.

length of wall, thousands of years old, and thousands of kilometers long, supposedly constructed to divide nomadic barbarians from the areas of cultivated Chinese centrality, is in fact a series of disjointed walls, tamped mounds, . . . and trenches."[9]

The Chinese developed techniques for building walls as early as the Spring and Autumn Period. The first scattered sections of what later became the Great Wall date to the Warring States Period of the Zhou dynasty during the fifth century BCE. These sections were built by various feudal states, including Qi, Yan, and Zhao, to defend against rival

A Dilemma at the Eastern Wall

The Great Wall had a mixed record as a fortification. Its earliest forms, featuring low earthen mounds and trenches, were vulnerable to invading forces on horseback or foot. Later dynasties built taller and thicker walls of masonry that presented a more formidable barrier. Nonetheless, the Great Wall was probably more effective as a psychological barrier and an emblem of Chinese power and wealth than as an actual military asset.

In 1644 the Great Wall seemed to be facing a crucial test when a certain decision changed history. General Wu Sangui was in command of eighty thousand Ming troops at Shanhai Pass, the easternmost part of the Great Wall. At that time rebels had seized Beijing, burning and looting the city, taking Wu's family hostage, and leading the Ming emperor to commit suicide. With the rebels approaching from the south and the powerful Manchus advancing from the north beyond the wall, Wu faced a dilemma. He decided to throw open the gate at Shanhai Pass and allow Prince Dorgon's Manchu armies through the Great Wall. Wu enlisted Dorgon's help in defeating the rebels and avenging his family. However, the price of his decision was the fall of the Ming dynasty. Ming partisans blamed Wu Sangui for handing over the empire to the Manchus. "And the Great Wall probably missed its last opportunity to show its worth," says journalist Riho Laurisaar. "Actually, quite the opposite—it was the last time the Great Wall got to prove that it was not of much use."

Riho Laurisaar, "The Failure of the Great Wall," Gbtimes, May 23, 2012. http://gbtimes.com.

states and marauding nomads in the north. Advances in architecture at the time had led to the construction of solid walls around major cities, especially capitals. The success of these city walls as protective measures prompted some warlords to build sections of wall outside their cities on borders and across open passes. These sections butted up against natural formations such as rivers, embankments, and steep mountain ridges to form effective barriers against enemy invaders. Since the walls had only to withstand attack by spears and swords, most were formed hastily by tamping down layers of earth and gravel between wooden planks. Many of these earliest sections, which originally lay north of the Great Wall that exists today, have been lost to centuries of erosion. What is left barely resembles a wall anymore. Instead, the remnants look like a rough earthen mound extended across the landscape.

In 221 BCE Qin Shi Huang defeated all rival states to unify China under the Qin dynasty. Qin territory expanded hugely, resulting in a long, porous border between northern China and the Mongolian plains. The new emperor knew he had to control this long border to protect against invaders and limit outside influences. He also wanted to unify people who had always been separated by boundaries of region and village. Qin Shi Huang directed his engineers to connect three main wall sections built by the Yan, Zhao, and ex-Qin states. Parts of these original walls were so weather-beaten or flimsy that they had to be rebuilt or reinforced. Surviving remnants of the Qin wall are about 20 feet (6 m) high and formed of blocks made from mud or the local stone. Laborers for this enormous project numbered more than 2 million, drawn from the armies of Qin Shi Huang's top general, Meng Tian. Work crews also included captured enemy soldiers and convicts from all over China. The first section of the Great Wall took ten years to complete and claimed the lives of countless workers. The Chinese people hated Qin Shi Huang's vanity and harsh rule and took little pride in his elaborate wall. They regarded it not as a symbol of strength or unity but rather as a source of misery for unlucky laborers.

The Han Additions to the Wall

Emperors of the Han dynasty made practical use of the wall concept. They linked long sections to the Qin wall, creating a new barrier that extended for 6,214 miles (10,000 km), the farthest extent of the Great

Wall in Chinese history. The Han wall, aimed at protecting the Silk Road trade to the west and preventing invasion from the northern Huns and Xiongnu, reached westward to Lop Nor in the rugged territory of modern-day Xinjiang. As always, the builders of the wall made use of local materials. In the western desert, where stone and wood were not available, the wall was made of sand, reeds, and branches of a desert shrub called the tamarisk. Mixing the hard-packed sand with water created a wall as hard as concrete. Branches and reeds also were lit on fire and used as beacons all along the western wall. The Emperor Wudi commanded that the finished wall should have a beacon every 5 *li*, a tower every 10 *li*, a fort every 30 *li*, and a castle every 100 *li*. (A *li* is a Chinese measurement of roughly 1,760 feet, or 536 meters.) Beacons of fire were used as warning signals at night, and columns of smoke served the purpose during the day. One smoke column indicated that a force of fewer than one hundred enemy troops had been spotted. Two columns meant the force numbered about five hundred and three columns warned of more than a thousand. The Han system of beacons could relay news more rapidly than a rider on a horse. Manned by alert sentries, the Han wall served as an early-warning system for signs of trouble on the frontier.

The dynasties that followed the Han, from the Sui to the Tang, Song, and Yuan, continued to repair, modify, and extend the Great Wall for defensive purposes. Sometimes these projects were done hastily, as if responding to a crisis. Chinese historians record that in July 607, the Sui emperor Yangdi commanded more than 1 million workers to build a wall eastward from present-day Yulin in Shaanxi Province to the bank of the Hun River. (Yangdi was accustomed to using armies of laborers to build his palaces and dredge his ornamental lakes.) The entire project was completed in ten days. In some places wall sections built by two separate dynasties run for an extended distance side by side.

The Walls of the Ming

The sections of the Great Wall that are most familiar today are mainly the work of the Ming dynasty. Archaeologists have found that the Ming walls extend more than 5,500 miles (8,851 km) east to west from the Yalu River in Liaoning Province to the east bank of the Tao-

Much of the Great Wall most familiar today was constructed during the Ming dynasty. Watchtowers like the one depicted in this twentieth-century illustration were large enough to provide living space inside for guards and sentries.

lai River in Gansu Province. A line of Ming emperors kept engineers and workers busy constructing and fortifying the walls to guard against invasion from deposed Mongol Yuan forces in the north and nomad tribes intent on raiding the empire. The Ming referred to the walls as border barriers, emphasizing their military purpose. In 1373 Emperor Hongwu set up eight border garrisons (troops stationed at an outpost) at the northern wall to discourage attacks from the frontier.

In the early 1400s Hongwu's son, Yongle, built walls of stone and earth with signal towers and trenches to fortify the border in strategic areas. Sometimes moats were added on both sides of the wall to slow invading forces. Yongle also moved the Ming capital to Beijing. Here, where securing the capital was of vital importance, the Great Wall was constructed in double lines of stone and earth to provide

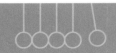
Today the Great Wall of China is a tourist attraction, commemorated in smartphone photos around the world. Some sections receive as many as seventy thousand tourists a day. Visitors stroll and strike poses along the crumbling stone ramparts where ancient Chinese sentries once trod. As photos reveal, the most frequently visited wall sections, such as those outside Badaling and Mutianyu, show definite signs of wear. According to a 2015 report by China's State Administration of Cultural Heritage, almost a third of the Ming-constructed wall has eroded away, and older sections are even more depleted. The revelation set off panicked reactions on social media worldwide.

There is no doubt that time, tourism, pollution, and weather are continuing to take a heavy toll on this vast artifact of Chinese history. As a result, the Chinese government is stepping in to preserve this cultural treasure. Regulations forbid tourists to remove pieces of the wall, and the regime has instituted programs to plant trees and shore up sloping sections that are most in danger of erosion. Yet in impoverished villages near the wall, bricks from the structure, some with Chinese words etched into them, are sold in local markets for less than ten dollars apiece. As one Chinese blogger writes, "The modern Chinese have done what people for centuries were embarrassed to do and what the invaders could not do. The wall is being destroyed by the hands of the descendants."

Quoted in Edward Wong, "China Fears Loss of Great Wall, Brick by Brick," *Sinosphere* (blog), *New York Times*, June 29, 2015. http://sinosphere.blogs.nytimes.com.

inner and outer security. Gates in the wall kept entry and exit in the open passes around the capital tightly controlled. Special garrisons manned watchtowers and observation posts along the wall's length. Overall, the Ming built hundreds of watchtowers along the length of the Great Wall. Unlike earlier outposts along the structure, which had been monoliths made of solid stone or dried mud, the Ming watchtowers were built as large shelters with living space inside for guards and sentries. These soldiers continued the practice of lighting fires as signal beacons when they spotted suspicious activity in the distance.

Sometimes, though, sentries fell prey to bribes, allowing enemy raiding parties to pass through the gates.

In 1449 a disastrous military defeat at the hands of the Mongols—including the capture of the Emperor Zhengtong—led the Ming to focus on preserving the empire and avoiding full-scale warfare. Reinforcements and additions to the wall became more elaborate as defensive measures. In the mid-1500s a military commander named Weng Wanda led a five-year project of unprecedented size to build and fortify sections of the wall in the region of Beijing. For the first time the wall was used to mount artillery and firearms loaded with Chinese gunpowder. Walls in some strategic areas were tripled or quadrupled in thickness and strength. Engineering on the additions to the wall was extraordinary. Laborers, including experienced masons, built sections using bricks and stone that had to be transported to the worksite at great cost. The later Ming additions to the Great Wall cut across wildly uneven terrain, giving it the appearance of a huge snake or dragon undulating through the rolling frontier.

The Legacy in Lives and Literature

Ultimately the wall failed to protect the Chinese from invasion. The Ming lacked money and troops to patrol the entire length of the wall. Mongols and Manchus simply attacked the wall at outposts where it was most lightly defended. The Great Wall "didn't do what it was supposed to do, it was enormously costly, and there's no question that it caused great suffering among the people who built it," says Arthur Waldron, an expert in Chinese history at the University of Pennsylvania. "In Chinese history, the wall has always been viewed negatively until the last century when it suddenly turned into a positive symbol of Chinese greatness. Before that it was always a symbol of futility, waste, cruelty, bad policy."[10]

The Ming never used the term *Great Wall* because they associated it with the heartless tyranny of the first Qin emperor.

> "[The Great Wall] didn't do what it was supposed to do, it was enormously costly, and there's no question that it caused great suffering among the people who built it."[10]
>
> —Arthur Waldron, professor of Chinese history at the University of Pennsylvania

The hardships suffered by workers on the wall are legendary. They toiled long hours in extreme temperatures and in remote, sometimes treacherous locations. Tradition has it that those who died from accidents, fatigue, or disease often were interred inside the wall. However, decomposing bodies would have destabilized the wall with air pockets, and archaeologists have discovered that bodies were actually buried in ditches alongside the wall. A common Chinese estimate is that at least four hundred thousand workers lost their lives building one or another of the many wall sections.

Chinese literature contains many descriptions of the workers' misery in poems and tales. One famous legend tells the story of Meng Jiangnu, whose husband is seized one night by officers of the Qin

These structures are forts that are part of the Great Wall at the Jiayuguan Pass. Legend has it that one brick left over from the wall's original construction remains at the gate to the pass.

dynasty and sent off to work on the wall. Desperate to learn what happened to her husband, Meng Jiangnu searches the countryside. By the time she reaches the wall construction site, he is already dead. Learning the truth, Meng Jiangnu howls in grief and causes a large part of the wall to collapse.

Another tale presents a clever worker who calculates that the wall at Jiayuguan Pass will require exactly 99,999 bricks. His cruel supervisor laughs and promises that if his calculation is off by even one brick, the whole crew will be sentenced to three years' hard labor. When the wall is finished at last, the supervisor is delighted to see that a single brick is lying at the gate to the pass. Before the supervisor can impose his punishment, the worker stops him by explaining that the brick was placed there by a supernatural spirit to make any future repairs. Should the brick be moved even slightly, he explains, the whole wall will tumble. According to the story, that brick still lies at the tower gate at Jiayuguan Pass.

The Great Wall was built as a promise of security and unity among the Chinese. Yet it also fostered a dangerous sense of isolation from the outside world. Later emperors tried to keep the world at bay and avoid contact with those outside China's borders, but this proved to be a shortsighted policy that discouraged foreign trade and sowed distrust among other nations. For all its grandeur, the Great Wall stands in many ways as a sign of failure.

CHAPTER THREE

What Effect Did Confucianism Have on the Chinese Moral and Political Outlook?

Focus Questions

1. Why do you think Confucius's teachings were so influential in ancient China? Explain your answer.
2. Why was Confucius's emphasis on scholarship so important to Chinese culture over the centuries? Explain your answer.
3. Do you think that a modern government could be successfully founded and run on Confucian ideas? Why or why not?

In 2013, when China's new president, Xi Jinping, announced his project to restore his nation to greatness, few expected those plans to include a return to Confucianism, a moral and political philosophy that dates back to several centuries before the Common era. Yet today experts on Confucius and his ideas are in great demand in China. In June 2015 the Chinese government brought in Wang Jie, a professor of ancient Chinese philosophy, to deliver a lecture on Confucianism to two hundred high-level officials meeting in Beijing. Under Chairman Mao Zedong (leader of China from 1949 to 1976) and his successors, Confucian quotes and concepts relating to family values and personal morality were scorned as relics of the feudal past. The Communist Party did its best to destroy these traditional teachings in favor of ideas from Karl Marx and Mao.

Now Xi Jinping is restoring Confucianism as a distinctively Chinese alternative to Western ideas of democracy and personal freedom. Classical texts like Confucius's *Analects* are once more featured in school curricula and entrance exams. Teachers must undergo training classes to enable them to teach ancient texts that are unfamiliar to them. The government is spending freely on related projects, such as an online library of classical writings and a $250 million museum of traditional culture that sits next to the Olympic Stadium in Beijing. "It's like the prodigal son returning," says Guo Yingjie, a professor of Chinese studies at the University of Sydney in Australia. "China has had more than a century of anti-traditionalism. Now they're heading in the opposite direction."[11] Once more, as it has down through the centuries, Confucianism is playing an important role in the workings of the Chinese state.

A Teacher and a Moral Philosopher

Kongfuzi, or Kung the Master, whose name is latinized as Confucius, was born in 551 BCE, during the Zhou dynasty. His birthplace was the city of Zou in Lu state—close to Qufu in present-day Shandong Province on China's northeastern coast. Confucius came from a ruined aristocratic family and was self-educated. His early years coincided with a tumultuous time in China, marked by feuding warlords who created their own states by force and oppressed the people with slave labor and heavy taxes.

As a young man, Confucius maintained the granary and supervised agriculture for a local noble. This activity spurred his interest in ethics and good government. Soon Confucius left his home territory to roam for several years through the states of China. He sought to share his philosophy with local rulers and encourage them to govern their people selflessly with policies based on virtue and the common good. His project proved to be naive when the warlords and princes he met sent him packing. Nevertheless, his vision of a life based on virtuous principles won the hearts of downtrodden people. Their support convinced him to return to his home state and become a teacher of young men, both rich and poor.

Confucius considered himself an instrument for passing on timeless ideas for living. He hoped that the training he offered in ethics, leadership, history, and psychology would prepare his students to take government positions and become the best sort of administrators, capable of transforming China with their merit and wise influence. "For Confucius, political meritocracy [government by those

Kongfuzi, or Confucius (pictured), was a teacher who developed a philosophy stressing the value of virtuous living. Many of his followers became government administrators whose adherence to this philosophy helped bring order to an era of crisis and chaos in China.

most qualified] starts from the assumption that everybody should be educated," says Daniel Bell, an expert on China and Confucianism. "An important task of the political system is to select leaders with an above average ability to make morally informed political judgments, as well as to encourage as many people of talent as possible to participate in politics. Such rulers, in Confucius's view, would gain the trust of the people."[12]

Confucius's success as a teacher and moral philosopher did indeed bring about change to China's government and institutions. His followers, armed with his teachings about proper behavior and ethical treatment of others, fanned out across China to become government officials in various states, just as he had dreamed. Confucian teachings helped bring order to a time of crisis and chaos. Accounts vary on whether Confucius himself served in government in his later years, but his ideas doubtless had an enormous impact on the way the Chinese people lived and were governed. That this self-taught man, steeped in a background of ancestor worship and with no knowledge of Greek philosophy or Jewish scripture, should transmit such a humane and influential system of his own is all the more remarkable.

> "An important task of the political system is to select leaders with an above average ability to make morally informed political judgments, as well as to encourage as many people of talent as possible to participate in politics. Such rulers, in Confucius's view, would gain the trust of the people."[12]
>
> —Daniel Bell, an expert on China and Confucianism

While teaching, Confucius also began to write, producing two collections of poetry and a history of the state of Lu, among other works. However, he never set down his ideas about life, family, and government in his own words. His legacy was left to others. When Confucius died in 479 BCE, he was widely recognized as a great teacher and philosopher. Yet he might have been surprised to learn that his philosophy based on ancient ideas would one day become virtually the state religion of imperial China.

The Basics of Confucianism

Although Confucianism is based on ancient Chinese religious principles, it is not strictly a religion. Its ideas were spread not through churches and pastors but through the common institutions of Chinese society, including the family, schools, and the government. Confucianism was woven into the routines of everyday life in China. It might be called a civil religion.

Living in chaotic times, Confucius sought to revive the ritual practices that in his view had made the Zhou dynasty and its unnamed religion such a success. These included not only ceremonies such as funerals and sacrifices to the dead but also the daily social rituals, such as being courteous to others and showing respect for one's elders. Each person had his or her defined role and obligations at home and in society. Conforming to one's role kept society operating in an orderly way. Confucius also believed that people are essentially good. Thus, any person who seeks knowledge and finds sound examples to follow can display ethical behavior. The importance of learning to an orderly society is described in a section of the *Book of Rites*:

> "Only when character is cultivated are our families regulated; only when families are regulated are states well governed; only when states are well governed is there peace in the world."[13]
>
> —Confucius

Only when things are investigated is knowledge extended; only when knowledge is extended are thoughts sincere; only when thoughts are sincere are minds rectified [kept to the right way]; only when minds are rectified are the characters of persons cultivated; only when character is cultivated are our families regulated; only when families are regulated are states well governed; only when states are well governed is there peace in the world.[13]

The stress Confucius placed on education led to the rise of a class of bureaucrats—some of whom were his former pupils—who were well educated, moderate in their personal behavior, and filled with a healthy respect for authority. Such officials helped run the government with great efficiency. The emphasis was on order, with the emperor at the top, ruling by way of the mandate of heaven. A cruel or inept ruler forfeited this mandate. For Confucius, a government that resorted to violence against its citizens was illegitimate and a failure.

Alongside social rituals, Confucianism stressed each person's *ren*, translated as "benevolence" or "goodness"—the ability to love and act humanely. The Chinese character for *ren* suggests the relationship between two persons, indicating how it involves conscience and doing right by others. For Confucius, a complete person has an inner life based on *ren* and an outer life guided by adherence to social rituals and courtesy. As written in the *Analects*, "[A person] should be earnest

Challenging Legalism

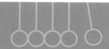

Before Confucius, the prevailing system of government in China was based on a school of thought called legalism. Despite its name, this philosophy emphasized rule by force, not law. Legalists believed that force was what people understood best. They insisted that people were evil by nature and that greed, jealousy, and selfishness would always lead them to act out of self-interest and never for the good of the community. To Legalists, people craved security above all but knew it had to come from a powerful ruler. Strict laws and harsh punishments were necessary to maintain order in society. Slight deviations would bring only chaos. Rule by legalism, with its brutal discipline, helped the Qin conquer other kingdoms.

Confucian ideas arose to challenge the Legalists' cynical attitude toward humanity. Confucius taught that people are inherently good and thus could be educated to hold positive values and to live by moral standards. These values could be spread through the home, the family, and the community, and thus throughout society. Rule by brute force, Confucius believed, with no allowance for compassion, must lead to widespread dissatisfaction and ultimate chaos. He advised looking back before legalism to the practices and traditions of China's golden age, which he considered to be the Chou dynasty.

However, legalism did not disappear. According to economist and historian Thayer Watkins, "Even after the fall of the Qin Empire and the rise of the Han Empire there were ministers who were ostensibly Confucian but who governed according to Legalist principles."

Thayer Watkins, "Legalism and the Legalists of Ancient China," San José State University. www.sjsu.edu.

and truthful, loving all, but become intimate with his innate good-heartedness."[14] Thus, Confucianism urged self-control, limits for self-interested actions, reverence for parents and ancestors, and treatment of others as one would like to be treated. Cultivating these ideas built character and formed the basis for a civilized society.

Spreading Confucian Ideas

Since Confucius failed to record his philosophy in written form, it was left to others to spread his ideas. Mostly this was done by government officials educated in Confucian principles. A few later disciples, such as Mencius and Xunzi, became philosophers in their own right. Mencius (390–305 BCE) refined the teachings of the master and made practical use of them by advising the king of Qi. He had a talent for creating allegories, or symbolic stories, to illustrate ideas. His popular proverbs, which condense Confucian ideas to memorable statements, include, "The great man is he who does not lose his childlike heart."[15] Mencius emphasized the Confucian teaching that human beings are basically good and merely need education and self-discipline to express their true nature. He valued the idea of a philosopher king—a wise ruler with his people's best interests at heart—but also believed that it was the duty of government ministers to revolt against an immoral ruler.

> "The great man is he who does not lose his childlike heart."[15]
>
> —Mencius, a disciple of Confucius

Mencius's philosophy was preserved in question-and-answer form in a text called *Mencius*.

Xunzi (310–220 BCE) did even more than Mencius to spread Confucian ideas throughout China. He systematized the ideas of Confucius and Mencius, giving them a coherent form that helped them survive for the next two thousand years. Yet Xunzi also departed from Confucianism in important ways. For example, he insisted that human nature is evil, lacking a moral compass and prone to fighting and disorder. He believed that rituals were necessary to curb human nature and bring order to society. Xunzi focused almost entirely on human beings and their role in making a better society rather than on the influence of heaven or the spirit world. To Xunzi, a good harvest resulted from a wise application of farming methods, not from heaven's favor. The key

A disciple of Confucius, Mencius (in yellow) went on to become a philosopher in his own right. In his teachings, he emphasized the Confucian principle that human beings are essentially good.

concept in his thinking is the Way, meaning the proper way of behaving or the ethical way of governing. This is a common idea in Chinese philosophy, although it is defined in different ways.

Confucian ideas also spread by way of texts. There are four texts considered to contain Confucius's principal teachings: *The Great Learning* and *The Doctrine of the Mean*, which are two chapters from

Confucius's *Book of Rites*; the *Analects*, a collection of sayings and proverbs that focuses on the moral virtues a noble person should follow, including benevolence and filial piety; and the *Mencius*, containing dialogues that illustrate Mencius's take on Confucian ideas. Of these four, the most revered text is the *Analects*.

Confucianism, as laid out in the *Analects* and other writings, became the dominant form of political thought during the Han dynasty. Thousands of academies produced students who carried this philosophy throughout China and eastern Asia. Although some rulers resisted Confucian ideas—Emperor Liu Bang supposedly would urinate in the hat of any visitor he pegged as a Confucian scholar—most welcomed the philosophy as a rational basis for good government.

The Rise of Competing Philosophies

Eventually the Han court succumbed to self-interest and political intrigue, leading to widespread chaos and the downfall of the Han dynasty. As a program for wise government, the influence of Confucianism declined. Many Chinese intellectuals decided that Confucian ideas, despite their moral appeal, had proved a failure in the real world. Large numbers turned to China's other two major schools of thought, some embracing Taoism, others Buddhism.

Taoism, which dates to the sixth century BCE, is said to have been founded by Laozi, who was a curator at the royal library in the state of Chu. A natural philosopher, Laozi supposedly lost patience with the corruption and selfishness he saw all around him. He decided to abandon the civilized world and go into exile. As he approached the western pass, the gatekeeper recognized him as a keen philosopher and begged him to write down his ideas before he left. As the story goes, Laozi sat down on a rock and composed the *Tao-Te-Ching*, or *The Book of the Way*. Handing his book to the gatekeeper, Laozi disappeared into the mists beyond the pass.

Whether or not Laozi really existed, the *Tao-Te-Ching* has survived to become influential not only in China but also worldwide. The book gathers poems and sayings—many based on ancient nuggets of folk wisdom—that insist that everything is interconnected. It suggests that individuals can achieve peace by following the Tao, or the Way, and always reckoning how their thoughts and acts affect

Laozi, the legendary founder of Taoism, is pictured in this eighteenth-century painting, accompanied by a disciple. The principles of Taoism are laid out in the *Tao-Te-Ching*, or *The Book of the Way*, which stresses the interconnectedness of all things.

not only themselves but others and the world. Whereas Confucianism preached duty and activity, Taoism urged inactivity and acceptance, merging with the world like a drop of water with the ocean.

Buddhism is based on the teachings of Siddhartha Gautama, the original Buddha, who lived in southern Nepal during the fifth century BCE. Siddhartha sought peace and salvation by way of meditating. For him, man's only hope of escaping life's misery was to undergo a series of reincarnations, or rebirths, until finally reaching the blessed end state of nirvana, which was nonexistence. A person earned merit by

Confucius on Tyranny

The Chinese philosopher Confucius insisted that a powerful ruler committed to the common good could change his subjects' lives for the better. He also warned of the reverse—a despot whose heartlessness brings misery and suffering. Confucius expressed this second idea with the proverb "Tyranny is fiercer than a tiger." The saying comes from a story told by Confucius's disciples.

As the story goes, Confucius and his followers were walking through the countryside when, at the foot of Mount Tai, they heard the sound of a woman weeping. Her mournful cries grew louder, echoing among the hills and caves around them. Confucius was curious as to what prompted her tears. He asked one of his disciples to seek out the lady and discover the reason for her anguished sobs. The disciple found her kneeling in a graveyard, beside a freshly dug grave. Between sobs the woman explained that a tiger had devoured her father-in-law, her husband, and now her son. The disciple offered his condolence but warned that her cries could bring the tiger back to claim another victim. He urged her to leave that barren place and return to her city. The woman replied that she could not afford the enormous taxes there and feared the ruler's cruel whims.

When his disciple passed on this explanation to Confucius, the great philosopher was struck by the old woman's reasoning. To his followers he said, "Keep it in mind, young fellows: tyranny is fiercer than a tiger."

Quoted in Sasha Astiadi, "A Proverb Explained: Tyranny Is Fiercer than a Tiger," *World of Chinese*, January 21, 2014. www.theworldofchinese.com.

obeying sacred rules against killing, stealing, lying, committing adultery, and drinking alcohol, and by rejecting worldly pleasures completely. A less stringent version, called Mahayana Buddhism, allowed for attaining salvation by way of sudden enlightenment. This form of Buddhism took hold in China around 220 CE and the fall of the Han dynasty. It grew even more rapidly during the political chaos of the Six Dynasties period (220–589), until it came to influence almost every part of Chinese culture.

Confucianism's Later Legacy

Confucianism did not disappear as other philosophies gained prominence. In fact Confucian ideas seeped into these other systems, especially Taoism. Most Chinese viewed the two philosophies as more complementary than antithetical. Officials could embrace Confucianism's practical approach to state affairs while also seeking the Way in their personal lives. The brief Sui reunification of China (581–618 CE) and the resulting prosperity helped revive a tradition of Confucian thought and scholarship. The Tang dynasty mixed Confucian ideas with its dominant Buddhism. Only in the later Song dynasty, however, did Confucianism regain its authority.

Confucianism's influence was not limited to China, spreading also to Japan, Korea, Vietnam, and other nations in eastern Asia. Yet Confucianism may also have played a part in China's isolation from the world, particularly during the Qing dynasty. Confucian beliefs, which held that Chinese society was whole and harmonious, worked against outside interference and foreign trade.

Mao Zedong's 1949 Communist revolution in China rejected Confucianism completely, although privately many Chinese continued to follow its age-old precepts. "Mao Tse-tung [Zedong] and Chou En-lai [first premier of the People's Republic of China] seem to have realized that Confucianism is still the ruling force in the hearts of the Chinese people and that Marxism is a veneer applied only for purposes of survival," wrote Liu Kang-sheng, a Taiwanese observer, in 1973. "The Chinese Communists have ample reason to fear Confucius and the Confucian influence. Master K'ung [Confucius] is as alive today as he was more than 2,500 years ago. He didn't contribute a religion and he didn't raise himself to the godhead, but he did shape a way of life for the world's most numerous people."[16] And today, in a major shift from past policy, the Communist Party in China is openly encouraging the people to embrace the ancient ideas of Confucius.

> "Master K'ung [Confucius] is as alive today as he was more than 2,500 years ago. He didn't contribute a religion and he didn't raise himself to the godhead, but he did shape a way of life for the world's most numerous people."[16]
>
> —Liu Kang-sheng, a Taiwanese commentator on Confucius

CHAPTER FOUR

How Did the Chinese Invention of Gunpowder Affect Warfare in the World?

Focus Questions

1. What effect do you think the first sight of exploding gunpowder had on the Mongols? Explain your answer.
2. Why do you think the Song government tried to keep gunpowder out of foreign hands? Explain your answer.
3. Did the invention of gunpowder make warfare worse? Why or why not?

Cai Guo-Qiang is a native Chinese artist who uses gunpowder as his medium. As director of visual effects at the 2008 Olympic Games in Beijing, Cai stunned a worldwide audience with his fireworks display called *Footprints of History* at the opening ceremony. It featured twenty-nine gigantic sparkling footprints, produced by fireworks and arrayed across the sky above the city. Cai intended the display as a tribute to China's rich history and culture, a history that includes the invention of gunpowder many centuries ago. The artist considers gunpowder as natural a medium for art as ink or paint. In fact, he has painted with gunpowder by sprinkling various grades of it on canvas and igniting it. The result is random, feathery blotches of brown and black—not so out of place in a modern art show. One reason he chose to work with gunpowder is the danger it represents. "What gunpowder gave back to me was destructive," he explained to the *New York Times*. "It could be completely annihilating. The day it no longer has that destructive power for me may be the point to exit this stage."[17] As Cai's work suggests, gunpowder has served as both a helpful tool and a destructive weapon down through the ages. It remains one of China's most consequential gifts to the world.

The Discovery of Gunpowder

Gunpowder, a substance so effective at shortening a life, was originally discovered during experiments aimed at extending human life forever. Around 142 CE, during the Han dynasty, a Chinese alchemist—a forerunner of a modern chemist, with a good deal of occult practice

Fireworks light up the sky over the National Olympic Stadium during the 2008 Beijing Olympic Games. With the development of gunpowder in approximately 850 CE, fireworks became a feature of Chinese celebrations and have remained so up to the present day.

thrown in—was the first to describe the basic makeup of gunpowder. Wei Boyang wrote about how a mixture of three powders would furiously "fly and dance."[18] Around 300 CE, the Taoist monk and scientist Ge Hong listed the three ingredients of gunpowder: saltpeter, sulfur, and charcoal. Ge Hong, a recluse who styled himself "the Master who embraces simplicity," stumbled on this concoction in his attempts to find a medicine that would give a person eternal life. Yet the importance of his discovery largely went unrecognized, and it was lost for centuries.

It was not until around 850 CE that later Chinese alchemists accidentally rediscovered the recipe. Like Ge Hong, they were tinkering with various ingredients in hopes of creating an elixir that would bestow immortality. Their work resulted in failure after failure, yet they refused to abandon such an important quest. Most of the failed mixtures contained saltpeter, or potassium nitrate. Natural crystals of potassium nitrate were collected from animal dung that had dried in fields and begun to decay. The crystals formed in the manure and could be drained off by washing a dried manure pile in cold water. The production of saltpeter requires a warm, tropical climate, as in China's southern region. (Historians speculate that this is one reason why the chemical mixture of gunpowder never occurred to northern Europeans.) The Chinese had been gathering saltpeter for centuries before the alchemists became interested in it. Among its useful properties is its ability to dissolve ores and to serve as a purifying agent in making metals. Saltpeter looks like other simple salts, but the Chinese learned to identify it with a flame test—it burns with a violet flame.

Chinese alchemists had known of pure sulfur, the next ingredient of gunpowder, since the second century CE. Sulfur was harvested by mining it from yellowish volcanic rock or by heating iron pyrite, or fool's gold. The third ingredient, charcoal, usually came from the willow tree, although other sources, such as hazel, elder, and pinecones, worked as well. In later versions, charcoal was replaced by coal dust or sugar to provide the necessary carbon. Ground together, the three substances formed a black powder called serpentine. The recipe called for about fifteen parts of saltpeter, three parts of charcoal, and two parts of sulfur. As the alchemists soon learned, mixing these ingredients together held wondrous possibilities but was also extremely hazardous. The gunpowder mixture burns rapidly. As it burns, it produces

There is a perception that the Qing dynasty lagged far behind Europe in gunpowder weaponry and military technology in general. Until the 1700s, however, Chinese cannons were superior to European models in many ways. Qing artillery pieces were lighter than European cannons, yet they could fire similar weights of ammunition. Qing light cannons were capable of a higher rate of fire, although at a reduced range. Lightness also meant greater mobility. The Qing could take apart their cannons with ease and haul them on horses or mules—and occasionally on camels. Cannons that were too heavy could be melted down close to the battlefield and recast to a smaller bore. Mobility enabled Qing forces to distribute more cannons per soldier than European armies of the time. For example, during the 1686 Siege of Albazin against the Russians, the Qing equipped 15,000 soldiers with 150 cannon. This ratio of 1 artillery piece per 100 troops was unmatched in contemporary European armies until the Napoleonic Wars of the early nineteenth century.

As for smaller arms, the Qing kept pace there as well. Military records show that for every one thousand soldiers, five hundred carried Portuguese muskets, three hundred were archers, and two hundred were infantry wielding swords and spears. Confucian reluctance to wage war might have limited the Chinese emphasis on cannons and firearms, but the idea that China somehow abandoned the technology for making gunpowder weapons is not borne out by the record.

hot gases that are greater in volume than the initial powder. The gases rapidly expand, causing an explosion.

Alchemists found out quickly that manipulating the powder around an open flame could be deadly. Taoist texts warned of the hazards of experimenting with serpentine, describing the blackened faces and singed beards of those whose tests had exploded in their faces. Even a random spark could be dangerous—although the early recipes for gunpowder apparently contained too little saltpeter to make the most explosive mixture. Alchemists began to mix the serpentine powder with water or wine for safety reasons. The pasty mixture then could be run through a screen to make small pellets, which could be dried for later use.

Fireworks and Other Uses

The Chinese alchemists' discovery was initially employed in fireworks. As early as 200 BCE, the Chinese had created a sort of primitive firecracker by roasting dried bamboo shoots, causing their hollow air pockets to explode with a pop. These firecrackers were used to frighten off evil spirits. With the invention of gunpowder, the Chinese created more powerful fireworks. They stuffed bamboo shoots with the volatile powder and hurled them into the fire. The louder the blasts became, the greater the cheers that erupted from onlookers. Soon *yan huo*—Chinese for "fireworks"—were being fired off to celebrate great events, such as a visit from the emperor. These magical displays included smoke trails, flames, colored wheels, kites propelled by fireworks, and showers of sparks that filled the sky. Inventors discovered that bamboo shoots could be replaced by gunpowder-filled paper tubes to fashion small rockets that would explode with even more startling force.

Gunpowder also was used to treat skin diseases and—perhaps in a mixture with arsenic or some other poison—to kill insects with smoky fumes. The Chinese were slow to realize the military uses of their discovery. However, at some point an unknown tinkerer produced a flaming arrow ignited with gunpowder or some other simple application. The sight of a fiery missile shooting across the sky must have seemed a revelation. The rush to find new ways to adapt gunpowder to the battlefield was on.

A Whole Arsenal of New Weapons

In 1040 CE, during the northern Song dynasty, a Chinese alchemist named Tseng Kung-Liang published a printed work titled *Wujing Zongyao*. In it he and his associates presented a detailed formula for gunpowder. He also was first to discuss the mixture's potential as a weapon. Tseng Kung-Liang described how different mixtures could be adapted for three kinds of weapons: a sort of smoldering smoke bomb, a flamethrower, and a hand grenade that produced a small explosion. Like the earlier alchemists, Tseng Kung-Liang's gunpowder lacked the three-quarters portion of saltpeter needed for a powerful detonation. That development had to wait for other Chinese scientists who drew upon his work. Yet Chinese soldiers were already learning to use so-called flying fire. These were arrows enhanced with narrow tubes of gunpowder that could be ignited and shot into enemy positions like small missiles.

Song-era inventors used gunpowder to create a whole arsenal of new weapons. For example, it became a vital part of siege warfare, in which a Song army would surround and blockade a city or town in an effort to capture it. Arrows fitted with packets of gunpowder were used as incendiary (fire-producing) weapons to set wooden structures on fire. A rocket launcher called the long serpent could fire about 320 arrows at one time from a series of small chambers. On the battlefield, soldiers would transport the launcher in a simple wheelbarrow. Balls made of scrap iron and gunpowder were lit on fire and lobbed with a catapult to batter enemy roofs and walls.

The Song also fashioned the first cannons, with vase-shaped barrels made of cast iron or bronze. Cast-iron cannonballs had a hollowed-out core that was filled with gunpowder in order to explode on impact.

Workers pose with a cannon and cannonballs at a Chinese armory in the late 1800s. By the time this photo was taken, cannons had been in use as artillery weapons in China for centuries.

A Chinese painting showing a working cannon dates from 1127 CE, more than a century before artillery pieces appeared in Europe.

Weapons of the Song dynasty demonstrated ingenious technology. Soldiers would carry so-called fire-spurting lances, or *huo chiang*, which were much like modern flamethrowers. This weapon consisted of a cylinder made of metal or bamboo and filled with a liquid fuel such as oil or naphtha. A double-piston arrangement could be triggered to pump oil out of the cylinder, whereupon a smoldering gunpowder fuse lit it afire. The fire lance produced a continuous stream of flame that could extend for several yards—certainly a terrifying prospect for an enemy soldier trying to climb a city wall. According to technology expert Joseph Needham,

> At first, fire lances were held manually by the fire-weapon soldiers, but by the time of the Southern Sung [Song] they were made of bamboo much larger in diameter, perhaps up to a foot across, and mounted on a framework of legs, sometimes even provided with wheels so as to make them moderately mobile. . . . Nothing or almost nothing like it existed in the Western world.[19]

The Song also developed primitive hand grenades, which were small ceramic or metal pots that were stuffed with gunpowder and shrapnel and hurled at the enemy. Song engineers even made exploding land mines that were activated by a trip wire. The Song laid these mines strategically across narrow passes to thwart the invading Mongols.

The Spread of Gunpowder Technology

Initially the Song's gunpowder weapons gave them an advantage over their Mongol enemies. One effect of these fiery, explosive munitions was to sow terror among opposing troops. According to science writer Heather Whipps, "The psychological effect alone of the mystifying new technology likely helped the Chinese win battles against the Mongols, historians believe."[20] Yet the battle-hardened Mongol warriors soon adapted to the situation. By stealing artillery pieces or seizing Song engineers and gunners, the Mongols were able to develop gunpowder-based weapons of their own. In this early arms race, the Song maintained their lead for decades due to their scientists' ingenuity and expertise with the substance. In the end, however, the Mongols' relentless attacks proved too much for the declining Song forces. "Eventually, the Mongols were able to capture Chinese artisans and use

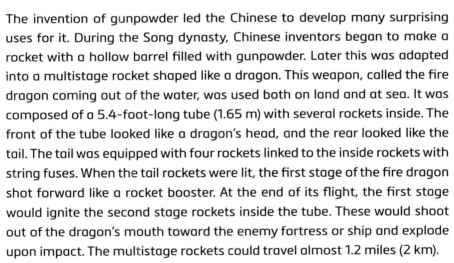

Gunpowder and Rockets

The invention of gunpowder led the Chinese to develop many surprising uses for it. During the Song dynasty, Chinese inventors began to make a rocket with a hollow barrel filled with gunpowder. Later this was adapted into a multistage rocket shaped like a dragon. This weapon, called the fire dragon coming out of the water, was used both on land and at sea. It was composed of a 5.4-foot-long tube (1.65 m) with several rockets inside. The front of the tube looked like a dragon's head, and the rear looked like the tail. The tail was equipped with four rockets linked to the inside rockets with string fuses. When the tail rockets were lit, the first stage of the fire dragon shot forward like a rocket booster. At the end of its flight, the first stage would ignite the second stage rockets inside the tube. These would shoot out of the dragon's mouth toward the enemy fortress or ship and explode upon impact. The multistage rockets could travel almost 1.2 miles (2 km).

Historians point out that Chinese experiments with rocketry led to, among other things, the internal combustion engine and space travel. "If we hadn't had [the first multistage rockets], maybe we would not have been able to put a man on the moon," notes Professor Robin D.S. Yates. "It was that fundamental an idea. . . . Our basic modes of transportation would not have been possible without this Chinese invention."

Quoted in *Nova*, "China's Age of Invention," PBS, February 29, 2000. www.pbs.org.

the latest gunpowder technology against the Chinese," says Professor Robin D.S. Yates. "The Mongols used those people who had a special knowledge of technology and employed them in their own armies as engineers. They carried that technology to the West very rapidly because it was very helpful in their conquests."[21]

Realizing the destructive power of gunpowder, Chinese rulers long had zealously guarded the secret of its manufacture. Selling the substance to foreigners was banned as early as 1076 CE. Yet news of this miraculous exploding powder was bound to escape the confines of imperial China. As the Mongols, led by Genghis Khan, pushed westward into Europe, they probably terrorized foes with their crude gunpowder-loaded cannons. The formula for gunpowder certainly found its way to India, the Middle East, and eventually Europe via the commerce along the Silk Road. It provided princes and warlords with the means to indulge their fantasies of conquest, and it tipped the scales on the moral basis for warfare. As Yates contends, "Gunpowder completely transformed the way wars were waged and contributed to the eventual establishment of might over right."[22]

> "Eventually, the Mongols were able to capture Chinese artisans and use the latest gunpowder technology against the Chinese. . . . They carried that technology to the West very rapidly because it was very helpful in their conquests."[21]
>
> —Robin D.S. Yates, professor of history and East Asian Studies at McGill University in Montreal, Canada

A New Kind of Warfare

Gunpowder technology arrived in Europe only in the late thirteenth century, making Europeans the last major group in the civilized world to unlock its secrets. First to publish the formula for gunpowder was a Franciscan monk in England named Roger Bacon. A scientist devoted to learning, Bacon was also known as Doctor Mirabilis, which was Latin for "Wonderful Teacher." In a text written in 1249, Bacon named the ingredients of so-called black powder, listed the proportions necessary for the mixture, and described its explosive potential. Bacon wrote in code to avoid the condemnation of the Catholic Church, which likely would have seen Bacon's work with a substance that produced, in his words, "thunder and lightning,"[23] as evidence of devil worship. Historians are not sure how Bacon obtained the Chinese formula for gunpowder. Some speculate it may have reached him from a soldier returned from the Crusades in the Middle East.

Once they became aware of its potential, Europeans wasted no time in adapting gunpowder to the battlefield. Early in the fourteenth century, European armies began to use the cannon, the most powerful weapon yet devised. It was a cylinder made of iron or bronze and closed off at one end. The cylinder was loaded with a charge of gunpowder and a cannonball. According to military historian J.B. Calvert, "When the charge was ignited through the touch-hole, it exploded, or changed to highly compressed gas, very quickly, expelling the ball to do whatever

English monk and scientist Roger Bacon (pictured) was the first to publish the formula for gunpowder. Although gunpowder technology did not arrive in Europe until the thirteenth century, armies quickly adapted it to the battlefield.

service was required of it. This service was smashing a wall, or dismembering men and horses, or crashing through the wooden side of a ship."[24]

With cannons in use and capable of battering down walls from a distance, medieval castles no longer offered protection from rival armies. One eventual effect of this change was to move battles away from fortresses and into open fields. By the middle of the fifteenth century, banks of cannons were often the deciding factor in military success.

> "When the charge was ignited through the touch-hole, it exploded, or changed to highly compressed gas, very quickly, expelling the ball to do whatever service was required of it."[24]
>
> —Military historian J.B. Calvert

Another gunpowder weapon revolutionized the role of the foot soldier. Around 1360, Europeans created their own version of the Chinese fire lance. These first primitive hand cannons were shot by lighting a wick connected to a touchhole in the barrel. This ignited the gunpowder inside, causing an explosion that fired a projectile. Within fifteen years, use of handguns had spread across Europe. Firearms made each soldier a deadlier adversary, even from long distance, like a mobile cannoneer. The Chinese invention of gunpowder had led to a new kind of warfare.

Gunpowder Technology Comes Full Circle

Europeans continued to make improvements in gunpowder and hand-held weapons. Corned gunpowder was refined by adding moisture to the mix and then drying it to make it densely grainy and significantly more powerful. European advances in metalwork enabled gunsmiths to manufacture rifles that were rugged and more durable and had a greater range. In the mid-1500s Europeans took this improved gunpowder technology back to China. Officials of the Ming dynasty allowed the Portuguese to set up a trading post on the empire's eastern shore, and the traders included firearms and artillery pieces among their wares. The Chinese, whose instinct was to resist outside influence, began to adopt European military technology simply to defend themselves. These new weapons proved to be a great deal more lethal than previous homegrown versions. The invention of gunpowder was a genie that could not be returned to the bottle.

CHAPTER FIVE

How Did the Silk Road Link China with the Rest of the World?

Focus Questions

1. What effect, if any, do you think the Silk Road might have had on China's political system?
2. What factors would have caused the Silk Road to reach its peak of prosperity? Explain your answer.
3. Do you think trade with other nations was necessary for a civilization like ancient China to achieve its potential? Why or why not?

In mid-December 2016, American satellite images revealed that China had installed antimissile and antiaircraft weapons on the South China Sea islands. The seven islands are artificial atolls created or enlarged by China's massive dredging projects. China intends to use the islands as a base for its control of the disputed waterways of the South China Sea. The United Nations' World Court has ruled against China's claims in this region. The dispute and arms buildup could threaten Chinese president Xi Jinping's massive effort to revitalize his nation's trade with Southeast Asia, the Middle East, and Europe. The plan, called One Belt, One Road, includes the Silk Road Economic Belt, an overland route through Eurasia that connects the Chinese industrial city of Xian with Tehran, Istanbul, Moscow, and Rotterdam, among other cities to the west. It also features the Maritime Silk Road Initiative, which links ports from Fuzhou and Guangzhou to Jakarta, Nairobi, Athens, and Venice.

Use of the term *Silk Road* is significant, as it refers to the fabled trade route that brought an end to China's isolation in the ancient world and linked the empire economically and culturally to the West. According to Christine Guluzian, an expert on China at the Cato Institute, the Chinese reaction to the World Court will be watched closely by its potential trading partners. "With its reputation regarding the rule of law at stake," says Guluzian, "China's handling of an international tribunal's ruling seems short-sighted at best. . . . China's response to the ruling is a litmus test providing an opportunity to demonstrate that it is a reliable partner in the new Silk Road, one committed to basing its 'win-win' (*shuang-ying*) policy on an adherence to the rule of law."[25] As in centuries past, China today seems to be struggling to balance its own security concerns with its desire to trade with the rest of the world.

A Historic Trade Route

The Silk Road was a trading route that developed in the second century BCE and lasted until the sixteenth century CE. The Silk Road was actually a network of roads—each one a well-traveled route between China and the West. The main route led from the western Han capital of Chang'an (now Xian) to central Asia and on to Persia and the eastern Mediterranean. Another important route wound south to the port in Hanoi, Vietnam, and then by sea via Indonesia and the Malay Peninsula to the Indian Ocean. In general, the Silk Road served to link ancient China with the Roman Empire and helped promote the circulation of goods and cultural traits among the civilizations of China, India, Persia, the Arab lands, Greece, and Rome.

It was China's most valuable export—the beautiful patterned silks coveted by merchants for centuries—that gave the historic trade route its name. In 1877 the German geographer and traveler Ferdinand von Richthofen coined the term *Silk Road* to emphasize the importance of the silk trade in bridging the cultures of East and West. The main

For centuries, silk was China's most valuable export, and the silk trade became a key factor in bridging the cultures of East and West. Here, workers weave the fabric, which is produced from the cocoons of silkworms.

artery of the Silk Road ran along the Persian Royal Road, an older route that went from northern Persia (modern-day Iran) to Asia Minor (today's Turkey) and the Mediterranean Sea. The Persian Royal Road was dotted with postal stations equipped with fresh horses for rapid delivery of messages. Maintained with care by the Persians, this road established the customary open access that was carried on by the Silk Road.

Beginnings in the Han Dynasty

China's first contact with the West took place around 130 BCE. Emperor Wudi of the western Han dynasty sought help in fending off nomadic tribes called the Xiongnu, who were repeatedly attacking the northern and western Han borders. The emperor sent his most trusted

Extraordinary Chinese Silks

The fabric the Silk Road is named for is extraordinary in many ways. It is among the softest and most comfortable of materials, and it is prized also for its shimmering, airy appearance. Chinese mastery of sericulture, or silk making, goes back thousands of years, with fragments of silk cloth found in southern China's Yangtze valley dating back to about 5000 BCE. Silkworms are found the world over, but among China's silkworms is a unique variety— a caterpillar with the scientific name *Bombyx mori* that is fed with mulberry leaves and produces silk of a rare quality. The hatched worm wraps itself in a cocoon made of a filament almost 1 mile (1.6 km) long and with amazing strength. The cocoons are boiled to kill the pupae within and to dissolve the gum resin keeping the filaments together. Filaments of several cocoons are then unwound, combined into a silk thread, and rewound onto a reel. Threads can be dyed—silk absorbs dyes especially well—and woven into rich fabric with intricate colors and designs. Making a dress requires 1 pound (0.5 kg) of silk, the product of about two thousand to three thousand cocoons.

Originally silk's elegance was reserved for the emperor's clothing. But use of silk eventually spread throughout Chinese society. "It also became a generalized medium of exchange, like gold or money," writes cultural anthropologist Richard Kurin. "Chinese farmers paid their taxes in silk. Civil servants received their salary in silk." And merchants along the Silk Road coveted the fabric as their most valuable item of trade.

Richard Kurin, "The Silk Road: Connecting People and Cultures," Smithsonian Folklife Festival. www.festival.si.edu.

general, Zhang Qian, on a journey westward beyond the Great Wall and through central Asia in search of assistance. Along the way Zhang Qian and his company of one hundred men met the Dayuan, a warlike people descended from the armies of Alexander the Great and living in what is now Uzbekistan. He admired the Dayuan's spirited, long-legged horses—known as celestial horses and believed to be related to those in heaven—which came from the Fergana valley of central Asia. The general saw at once that the steeds would prove enormously useful to Han cavalry in battling the Xiongnu raiding parties. "The general commandeered 3,000 of the finest stallions and mares," writes Audrey Topping, a historian of China,

> and reached an agreement that Ferghana would send two Celestial Horses each year to the Han emperor, along with enough seed to grow alfalfa for their nourishment. The stately caravan of heavenly horses trooped back along the Silk Road to the Han court, but only 1,000 of the strongest survived the long journey through the Hexi Corridor [through Gansu Province].[26]

Zhang Qian's mission—a perilous journey lasting thirteen years and costing the lives of all his men but one—proved a success when the Fergana horses he brought back tipped the balance against the Xiongnu. Soon the Han implemented a program to breed the new horses throughout the empire.

Zhang Qian also told stories of other previously unknown kingdoms he had encountered on his travels in Uzbekistan, including Samarkand and Bukhara. Emperor Wudi, intrigued by the general's tales and the opening to the West, wondered what other marvelous items might be obtained through trade. He sent Zhang Qian on another trip westward, this time with cattle, sheep, gold, silk, and other gifts for the rulers of the western kingdoms. It was the beginning of regular diplomatic missions and trading forays along the Silk Road. Exhausted by his efforts for Emperor Wudi, Zhang Qian died immediately upon his return from this second journey. Chinese historians honor Zhang Qian as the founder of the western trading routes. Centuries of Chinese poets and artists have based works on the general's exploits along the Silk Road.

Wudi also sent his armies into the northwest, beyond the Great Wall. His conquests in the West brought new lands into the Chinese sphere of influence, including the central Asian settlements of

> "The stately caravan of heavenly horses trooped back along the Silk Road to the Han court, but only 1,000 of the strongest survived the long journey through the Hexi Corridor [through Gansu Province]."[26]
>
> —Audrey Topping, historian of China

the Tarim Basin. The resulting Silk Road trade was a bonanza for governments and individuals from Chang'an to Egypt, Greece, and Rome. In exchange for their fabulous silks, Han traders first obtained horses, cattle, hides, and furs from central Asia and then broadened their commerce to include sesame, alfalfa, cucumbers, grapes, pomegranates, and walnuts. Luxury goods, such as fine linens and wools, jade, pearls, glass, and coral, began to flow eastward from India, Persia, and Arabia.

But the Silk Road provided more than trade and riches. A flood of foreign visitors to the Han territories brought with them a wealth of languages, customs, new ideas, and technical skills. Craftspeople passed along their own distinctive ways of building things and making art objects, such as sculptures and jewelry. Buddhist missionaries from India spread their religious philosophy, which mixed well with Confucianism and Taoism and soon developed deep roots. The Chinese discovered there were other civilizations in the world of comparable worth to their own—a shocking revelation for a people who had been isolated for so long.

A Peak of Prosperity

To preserve this valuable new influx of trade and ideas, Han rulers took steps to defend the Silk Road. Chinese troops repeatedly fought the eastern European Huns and other nomadic groups determined to take over the route. Around 60 BCE the Han set up the Protectorate of the Western Regions, a military outpost in Wulei that supervised the northwest portion of the Silk Road and kept the route open and thriving. At intervals along the trading route, the Han built beacon towers, manned by the military, which communicated by means of flags and fires.

However, the Han dynasty fell into decline, mainly due to the cost of Wudi's aggressive wars. It was not until the beginning of the Tang dynasty around 618 CE that Chinese dominance once more extended into central Asia. Emperor Taizong's armies conquered the western Turks and occupied numerous trading centers. Peace with Tibet was accomplished by offering its king the hand of a Tang princess in marriage. Taizong rose to power because of his military prowess and diplomatic skill, but it was his intelligence and open-mindedness that made him a great leader. Taizong established a government that promoted tolerance of outside ideas and curiosity about the world. Influenced by Taizong's humane rule—and defended by his soldiers—the Silk Road trade revived to reach a peak of prosperity beyond even that of the Han dynasty. Once again a fabulous variety of goods and ideas began to circulate along the trade routes. Chinese traders exchanged silks, paper, ceramics, and tea for all manner of foreign goods, knowing they would bring an even greater price back home.

Under Taizong, the Tang capital of Chang'an became the world's largest, most sophisticated city, home to more than 2 million people. Attracted by Silk Road tales of China's incredible wealth, travelers and merchants from distant lands, including Japan, central Asia, Persia, and India, crowded into the city's streets and squares. Dark-bearded wine sellers offered their vintages from goatskin bags. Northern visitors with blond hair attracted delighted glances. Monks and pilgrims of different faiths padded along in sandals and simple tunics. Upper-class Chinese flaunted their foreign-made jewelry and exotic art objects, wore Western-style clothing with leopard-skin hats and narrow sleeves, and indulged in new pastimes. According to art historian Heather Colburn Clydesdale, "Polo and archery contests,

Trade languished during the waning years of the Han dynasty but was revitalized with the rise of the Tang dynasty. This illustration depicts workers transporting Chinese ceramics—which were an important medium of trade—to market in a wagon.

musical instruments and styles, and the scandalous Sogdian whirling dance were imported from kingdoms of Central Asia and fervently embraced in Chinese avant-garde circles."[27] The Sogdians were Persian Silk Road merchants who specialized in cultural exchange, including new kinds of music and styles of dress. Turkish folk songs and central Asian harp players and dancers became popular in Chinese cities. There was also a vogue for foreign recipes, such as various kinds of cakes sprinkled with sesame seeds and fried in oil. Spicy dishes made with expensive ingredients from other lands were special favorites.

> "Polo and archery contests, musical instruments and styles, and the scandalous Sogdian whirling dance were imported from kingdoms of Central Asia and fervently embraced in Chinese avant-garde circles."[27]
>
> —Art historian Heather Colburn Clydesdale

Overall, the era of Emperor Taizong and his successors was marked by confidence in traditional Chinese culture and keen interest in other cultures. Art historians note how Tang ceramic figurines are livelier in their poses and gestures than the stiff shapes of figurines from previous dynasties. Many of the figurines depict foreigners in their characteristic clothing. Tang artists also liked to draw upon other cultures to create fantastic mythical ceramic creatures with bright three-color glazes. These trends undoubtedly received a boost from the Silk Road trade and its jumble of influences.

The Decline of Foreign Influence

The Tang dynasty under Emperor Taizong represented a high point of interaction with foreign cultures. Li Cheng Qian, Taizong's eldest son and heir, comported himself as a Turkish nomad, wearing Turkish clothes and speaking only the Turkish language. By contrast, most foreigners who poured into Chinese cities from the Silk Road adopted Chinese habits and customs. There were no laws against intermarriage. Many Arab merchants married Chinese women, although they were not permitted to take them back to their homelands. For more than a century, the Chinese enjoyed generally peaceful relations with foreign visitors.

However, conflicts arose by the late 700s, especially with traders among the Uigur, who were a mixture of Mongol, Turk, and Tungus peoples (nomads of eastern Siberia). A law from 779 forbade Uigurs to wear Chinese clothing, marry Chinese women, or pose as native Chinese. Fifty years later, all private dealings with outsiders became illegal. In 845 the Chinese government acted to wipe out foreign influence altogether by persecuting foreign religions, especially Buddhism. Chinese troops destroyed thousands of Buddhist temples and sent

Chess and the Silk Road Influence

Along with a variety of goods, the Silk Road helped spread cultural ideas and customs. These included languages, religious practices, artistic forms, styles of dress and music, and favorite pastimes. The game of chess certainly owed its early expansion to merchants and travelers on the Silk Road. Chess scholars disagree about the origins of the game. "The idea of it being a combination of elements from other board-games has merit," says Silk Road scholar Horst Remus, who stresses its Indian roots. Some trace modern chess to a game from northern India called *ashtapada* that featured a square board divided into sixty-four squares. Others suspect that the game was invented in China. However they came to be, early forms of chess spread along the Silk Road among merchants who spent many hours in each other's company. Playing games became one way of developing bonds of trust.

Over the centuries, variations of chess fanned out from China and India to Persia and westward to Europe. Chess took on aspects of each new culture where it was introduced. An early version in India was played with dice, but this changed when Hindu law forbade gambling with dice. Pieces originally called elephants, which came from India and from the ancient game of *xiangqi* (Chinese for "elephant game"), became bishops in the Catholic West. A male piece known as the king's adviser became the queen, the most powerful piece in the European game. The Silk Road helped make chess a unique blend of many cultures.

Horst Remus, "The Origin of Chess and the Silk Road," *Silk Road Foundation Newsletter*. www.silkroadfoundation.org.

hundreds of thousands of nuns and monks into the countryside. Emperor Wuzong (840–846) turned to Taoism as the true Chinese faith, but Confucianism was also protected. As Buddhist influence declined, Islam became the dominant religion in areas to the west of China. These developments ushered in a long period of disrupted trade along the Silk Road.

Revival by the Mongols

It was not until 1271, and the rise of the Yuan dynasty of the Mongols, that the Silk Road once again flourished. Emperor Kublai Khan ordered the destruction of tollgates along the trading route and set up patrols to foil bandits, which led to safer and more convenient travel. Mongolian control boosted the caravan trade from China to the Mediterranean. Once again colored silks, now often patterned with threads of gold, became almost like currency in their value for trade. John Masson Smith Jr., a professor of Chinese history at the University of California–Berkeley, describes how the Mongols found new ways to expand the silk trade:

> [The Mongols] established new silk factories, in inner Mongolia, the Tarim Basin, and two in China proper, to increase the volume of silk production, and to develop new silk products. Chinese weavers were sent to Samarkand to collaborate with the local Muslim weavers, and Muslim weavers who were specialists in cloth-of-gold were brought to China. Wealthy Mongols invested in these enterprises, and in the vending of their products, forming commercial associations (*ortaqs*) with merchants experienced in transporting over the Silk Road, for instance, but also by sea and exchanging these goods abroad.[28]

The Mongols also added southern routes to the Silk Road, enabling caravans to avoid marauding nomads in the north by sweating through desert travel. Under the Mongols, expensive silks reached as far west as Italy, as did stories about the Chinese and their customs. At first the tales included outlandish descriptions of

Thirteenth-century Italian trader Marco Polo is depicted arriving in Beijing on horseback. He and other travelers returned to Europe with stories of China's natural beauty, extensive culture, and willingness to trade with Western merchants.

monsters and freaks, but eventually Europeans learned, from Marco Polo and other travelers, the truth about the Chinese empire—its immense size, its huge populations, its vast wealth, its distinctive and sophisticated culture, and its willingness to trade with the West on a forthright basis.

Replacement by Sea Routes

Ultimately, the overland Silk Road declined when traders in the West turned to travel by sea to reach China and India. Ships offered greater speed, more room for carrying goods, and less overall expense per voyage. In addition, the Ming dynasty increasingly turned inward, rejecting outside influence and viewing foreigners with suspicion. By the 1500s, the formerly prosperous southern routes and settlements had been swallowed by desert sands. The later Silk Road existed mainly as high mountain trails between Afghanistan, China, Pakistan, and India. These mountain routes continued in use until the early years of the twentieth century.

"For many in the region, the Silk Road is a story of peaceful trade, and a rich history of religious and harmonious cultural exchange."[29]

—Political journalist Tim Winter

The last decades of the Silk Road saw a new kind of traveler: people of science such as geographers, archaeologists, and mapmakers keen to explore the history of the route. These experts documented how the Silk Road did as much to spread ideas as to facilitate trade. As the political journalist Tim Winter notes, "For many in the region, the Silk Road is a story of peaceful trade, and a rich history of religious and harmonious cultural exchange."[29]

SOURCE NOTES

Introduction: The Terra-Cotta Army

1. Arthur Lubow, "Terra Cotta Soldiers on the March," *Smithsonian Magazine*, July 2009. www.smithsonianmag.com.
2. Quoted in *Nova*, "China's Age of Invention," PBS, February 29, 2000. www.pbs.org.

Chapter One: A Brief History of Ancient China

3. Quoted in Eric Jackson, "Sun Tzu's 31 Best Pieces of Leadership Advice," *Forbes*, May 23, 2014. www.forbes.com.
4. Quoted in Ann Paludan, *Chronicles of the Chinese Emperors: The Reign-by-Reign Record of the Rulers of Imperial China*. London: Thames & Hudson, 1998, p. 16.
5. Quoted in Shen Yun Performing Arts, "The Great Classic: Romance of the Three Kingdoms." http://cs.shenyunperformingarts .org.
6. Richard Hooker, "The Decline of the Ming." http://richard-hook er.com.

Chapter Two: How Important Was the Great Wall in the Development of Ancient Chinese Civilization?

7. Quoted in American Presidency Project, "Richard Nixon: Exchange with Reporters at the Great Wall of China—February 24, 1972." www.presidency.ucsb.edu.
8. Paludan, *Chronicles of the Chinese Emperors*, p. 19.
9. *China Heritage Quarterly*, "Length Does Matter," no. 6, June 2006. www.chinaheritagequarterly.org.
10. Quoted in James West, "Donald Trump Loves the Great Wall of China. Too Bad It Was a Complete Disaster," *Mother Jones*, March 3, 2016. www.motherjones.com.

Chapter Three: What Effect Did Confucianism Have on the Chinese Moral and Political Outlook?

11. Quoted in Jeremy Page, "Why China Is Turning Back to Confucius," *Wall Street Journal*, September 20, 2015. www.wsj.com.

12. Quoted in Emilie Frenkiel, "Choosing Confucianism: Departing from the Liberal Framework. An Interview with Daniel A. Bell," October 18, 2012. https://danielabell.com.

13. Quoted in Judith A. Berling, "Confucianism," Center for Global Education. http://asiasociety.org.

14. A. Charles Muller, trans., *The Analects of Confucius*. www.acmuller.net.

15. Quoted in Beyond Quarter Life, "The Great Man Is He Who Does Not Lose His Childlike Heart," January 11, 2015. http://beyondquarterlife.com.

16. Liu Kang-sheng, "Why Mao Hates Confucius," *Taiwan Review*, November 1, 1973. http://taiwantoday.tw.

Chapter Four: How Did the Chinese Invention of Gunpowder Affect Warfare in the World?

17. Quoted in Arthur Lubow, "The Pyrotechnic Imagination," *New York Times*, February 17, 2008. www.nytimes.com.

18. Quoted in Epic Fireworks, "History of Gunpowder." https://epicfireworks.com.

19. Joseph Needham, *Science in Traditional China: A Comparative Perspective*. Boston: Harvard University, 1981, pp. 41–42.

20. Heather Whipps, "How Gunpowder Changed the World," LiveScience, April 6, 2008. www.livescience.com.

21. Quoted in *Nova*, "China's Age of Invention," PBS, February 29, 2000. www.pbs.org.

22. Quoted in *Nova*, "China's Age of Invention."

23. Quoted in Royal Society of Chemistry, "Did You Know?: About Blackpowder." www.rsc.org.

24. J.B. Calvert, "Cannons and Gunpowder." https://mysite.du.edu/~jcalvert/tech/cannon.htm.

Chapter Five: How Did the Silk Road Link China with the Rest of the World?

25. Christine Guluzian, "Does the South China Sea Spell Trouble for Beijing's New Silk Road?," *National Interest*, August 16, 2016. http://nationalinterest.org.

26. Audrey Topping, "On the Old Silk Road with China's 'Celestial Horses,'" *Wag Magazine*, March 31, 2015. www.wagmag.com.
27. Heather Colburn Clydesdale, "Internationalism in the Tang Dynasty (618–906)," Metropolitan Museum of Art. www.metmuseum.org.
28. John Masson Smith Jr., "The Mongols and the Silk Road," *Silk Road Foundation Newsletter*. www.silkroadfoundation.org.
29. Tim Winter, "One Belt, One Road, One Heritage: Cultural Diplomacy and the Silk Road," *Diplomat*, March 29, 2016. http://thediplomat.com.

Books

Marcie Flinchum Atkins, *Ancient China*. Minneapolis, MN: ABDO, 2015.

Valerie Hansen, *The Silk Road: A New History*. New York: Oxford University Press, 2012.

Cindy Jenson-Elliott, *Ancient Chinese Dynasties*. San Diego: ReferencePoint, 2015.

Julia Lovell, *The Great Wall: China Against the World, 1000 BC–AD 2000*. New York: Grove, 2007.

Yuri Pines, *The Everlasting Empire: The Political Culture of Ancient China and Its Imperial Legacy*. Princeton, NJ: Princeton University Press, 2012.

Michael Schuman, *Confucius: And the World He Created*. New York: Basic Books, 2015.

Internet Sources

Andrew Browne, "China's Great Wall of Confrontation," *Wall Street Journal*, June 28, 2016. www.wsj.com/articles/chinas-great-wall-of -confrontation-1467090705.

Field Museum, "China's First Emperor and His Terracotta Warriors," March 4, 2016. www.fieldmuseum.org/discover/on-exhibit/warriors.

Arthur Lubow, "Terra Cotta Soldiers on the March," *Smithsonian Magazine,* July 2009. www.smithsonianmag.com/history/terra-cotta -soldiers-on-the-march-30942673.

Jeremy Page, "Why China Is Turning Back to Confucius," *Wall Street Journal*, September 20, 2015. www.wsj.com/articles/why-china-is -turning-back-to-confucius-1442754000.

Michael Schuman, "China's New Silk Road Dream," *Bloomberg Businessweek*, November 25, 2015. www.bloomberg.com/news/arti cles/2015-11-25/china-s-new-silk-road-dream.

Websites

China Highlights (www.chinahighlights.com). This travel-related website also contains excellent short articles on the history of ancient China. Topics include the significant accomplishments of various dynasties and the history of the Great Wall. The site also features excellent photographs of Chinese historical sites and cultural artifacts.

East West Dialogue (http://east_west_dialogue.tripod.com). This website is devoted to examining the cultures of China and the West, with a focus on how the two cultures share basic philosophical principles. Recent articles on the site look at ancient Chinese technology and the history of Confucianism.

History World (www.historyworld.net). The History World website includes an excellent section on ancient Chinese history, including links that take the reader to articles on such topics as Confucius, ancestor worship, Kublai Khan, and the Great Wall.

Silk Road Foundation (www.silk-road.com). This website promotes itself as "the bridge between eastern and western cultures." It features a wealth of information about the Silk Road, including a history of silk in China, maps of Silk Road routes, a chronology of Silk Road trade, a review of the famous travelers along the historic Silk Road, and other topics.